BY THE WATERS
OF LIVERPOOL

Helen Forrester was born in Hoylake,
Cheshire, the eldest of seven children, and
Liverpool was her home for many years
until she married. For the past thirty years
she has made her home in Edmonton,
Alberta. She has travelled widely in
Europe, India, the United States and
Mexico.

Helen Forrester is particularly well
known for her books about Liverpool: her
autobiographical books, *Twopence to Cross
the Mersey*, *Liverpool Miss*, *By the Waters of
Liverpool* and *Lime Street at Two* are all
available in Fontana, as are her novels,
some of which are also about Liverpool.

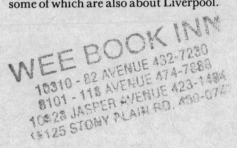

HELEN FORRESTER

By the Waters
of Liverpool

FONTANA/COLLINS

First published by The Bodley Head Ltd 1981
First issued in Fontana Paperbacks, 1983
Seventeenth impression May 1989

Copyright © Jamunadevi Bhatia 1981

Printed and bound in Great Britain by
William Collins Sons & Co. Ltd, Glasgow

The authors is most grateful to Naomi Lewis for
suggesting the title of *By the Waters of Liverpool*.

To dear Robert
who helped so much

Chapter one

I was seventeen going on eighteen, and I had never been kissed by a man. It was not surprising. Who would want to court the favours of a gaunt, smelly beanpole? I was five feet four inches tall, and that was real height in underfed Liverpool.

As I strode primly along Lime Street, on my way to evening school, the men who hung about the entrances of the cinemas hardly spared me a glance. I was most unflatteringly safe. And this, in a world where women still took it for granted that they would get married, was very depressing. Girls did not look for careers – they worked until they got married. If a woman was not loved and cherished by a man, she must be hopelessly ugly or there must be something else wrong with her.

I tried not to care that no young man had so much as winked at me. I stuck my proud Forrester nose in the air and vowed to make a career for myself as a social worker in the charity which employed me. Dorothy Parker, the famous American writer, had once remarked that men seldom make passes at girls who wear glasses; and I had a pair of too-small horn-rimmed spectacles perched on my nose. There was nobody to suggest to a shy, short-sighted girl that she might occasionally take off the ugly impediment to show the sad, green eyes behind.

'Perhaps your yellow skin will improve, as you get older,' my childhood Nanny, Edith, had suggested; and she scrubbed my face harder still with Pear's Preparing To Be A Beautiful Lady soap. To no purpose. All time and our subsequent poverty had done was to add a revolting array of acne spots, spots that were made worse by the lack of soap, hot water and clean towels at home.

And here was the year 1937 rolling along. Soon I would be eighteen. And nobody, I felt, really cared what happened to me. To my mother I was a trying daughter who brought in a wage each week; to the rest of the family a pair of hands, very useful for cooking and darning socks.

It was seven years since Father had gone suddenly bankrupt, plunging us into a poverty so great that I was frequently surprised that the nine of us had survived it, seven skinny children of whom I was the eldest, and two equally thin parents.

I sighed as I trudged up the hill. Though Mother and Father now both had work, they were very poor managers, and we were still cold and hungry most of the time, surrounded by the unpleasant odour of neglect and poor nutrition.

I handed my small wages to Mother every pay day, except for three shillings and sixpence. This totally inadequate sum was supposed to clothe me, pay for lunches and tram fares, make-up and all the small things a girl at work was expected to have. Mother was bent on making me give up my employment and once again stay at home to keep house, something I dreaded; so she made it as difficult as possible for me to go to work.

I found pupils to coach in shorthand in the evenings, but I earned very little because my free time was extremely limited.

I was doing very well at evening school, I comforted myself. One day I might be promoted and earn enough to live on. My ugly, kind bookkeeping teacher had assured me recently that, if I took one more course, I would be able to become a bookkeeper. She had added that parents were always glad of a girl at home who brought in a wage; it contributed to their comfort in their old age.

She had put into words something I dreaded, something only a husband could save me from. I could be faced with spending the rest of my life maintaining and waiting on two irritable, shiftless, nagging parents, the usual fate of the daughter who did not marry. Because I was plain and shy and frightened of my mother, I knew I could be bullied into being a nobody, a nothing.

Some women with gentle parents found their care a labour of love. Not me. I knew I would be crushed as flat as a shadow. I had already had a spell as housekeeper, from the age of eleven until I was fifteen. It had been a nightmare, looking after six young children and two quarrelling parents. Mother had, before Father's bankruptcy, never had to care entirely for her children. We had had servants. In fact, I hardly knew her until we were plunged into a slum together. She escaped from her unruly brood by working as a demonstrator in department stores.

9

In a frantic effort to escape myself, I had at the age of fourteen raged and threatened, as only a fourteen-year-old can, until I got permission to attend evening school, to repair in some part my lack of education.

At fifteen, with the unexpected help of Miss Ferguson, a deaconess at the local church, I had fought another battle to take the job I at present held. House-keeping was divided between a very angry mother and me.

I called Miss Ferguson my Fairy Godmother, and it was of this devout, cultivated lady that I was thinking, as I kicked a stone up Copperas Hill on the way to evening school. The street was quiet in the fading spring light, the misty air balmy – and I was shivering with pure fright.

Miss Ferguson had laid on my shoulders a fear worse than that of death, the fear of hell, Dante's hell.

How could she do such a thing? I wondered miserably, with a superstitious shudder. She was my Fairy Godmother.

She had first visited the family in order to recruit my two middle brothers, Brian and Tony, into the church choir. She knew them because all the children attended the church school. She had seen my situation as unpaid maid-of-all-work, and, perhaps to give me an hour or two of rest, she had pressured Mother into allowing me to go to church on Sunday evenings. At first I had no suitable clothes to go in, but once I could look at least neat, I thankfully attended.

We were Protestants, an important point in a city where the division between Protestants and Catholics was bitter and sometimes bloody. Children were aware from the time they could speak which side of the fence they stood on, and the implanted bigotry is to this day not entirely rooted out.

No amount of churchgoing could erase the vaguely erotic dreams which haunted me occasionally, or a terrible sense of empty loneliness. Ignorant, innocent, half-starved, practically friendless, my flowering body was trying to tell me of needs of which I had little notion. Almost all the myriad of novels I had read ended with the hero kissing the heroine for the first time. I had never considered what happened next. I felt a kiss would be the ultimate height of happiness.

But it was churchgoing which was causing my present unhappiness. As I turned into the big, gloomy evening school, which I loved so much, I was trembling with fear. Unable to concentrate on the shorthand teacher's rapid dictation, my mind was filled with scattered pictures of what had happened the previous Sunday.

Unaware of impending trouble, I had crept out of the back pew in which I normally hid my shabbiness, and battled my way up Princes Avenue through a brisk north-westerly carrying with it a spray of rain.

I was going home to a mother almost unhinged by her fall from considerable affluence, and to a fretful, delicate father, an under-paid, overworked city clerk. Liverpool was awash with the unemployed and the under-paid, and this governed all our lives. To a plain girl hurrying through the dusk, life seemed very hard. There was little physical strength in me. I was frail and always hungry, and I hugged my worn brown coat tightly round me for comfort.

Thankfully I pulled the string hanging from the letter-box of our row house. The latch lifted, and I was glad to step inside, away from the wind.

Miss Ferguson, Fairy Godmother and deaconess of the church, was seated in our old easy chair by the fire in our living room, undisturbed, it seemed, by the fetid atmosphere and the dirty chaos surrounding her. She must have been quicker than me in leaving the service and making her way over to our house, because she was already deep in conversation with Mother as I edged my way into the cluttered room. Her square pallid face with its cherry-red nose wrinkled up into a smile as I entered.

'Good evening, Helen.'

'Good evening, Miss Ferguson. Hullo, Mother.'

Mother was seated on a straight-backed chair opposite Miss Ferguson, and was smoking with long, deep puffs, the smoke like a fog round her head. Miss Ferguson seemed to be the only person able to penetrate beyond Mother's polite façade and fight her way through to the real, suffering woman beneath, and Mother was listening intently as Miss Ferguson continued their conversation.

Dressed in black, with wrinkled woollen stockings and flat-heeled shoes, her hair covered by a black coif, Miss Ferguson was very different from Mother's fashionable friends of so many years ago. But she was a cultivated woman, like my convent-bred mother, and it was a pleasure to listen to the hum of her soft voice.

I picked up an old fruit basket full of mending from beside the hearth and began my nightly task of darning the family's socks and stockings. Everybody's woollen socks or rayon stockings seemed to spring a hole or a ladder each day, and because we had so few pairs, they had to be darned ready for wear the next day.

At first, as my needle flew in and out, I did not take much notice of the conversation. Then Mother's voice penetrated. She sounded pettish. 'Helen's at evening school three times a week. And she is often out on Saturday evenings – either at the theatre with her friend, Sylvia, or teaching her shorthand pupil. Then church on Sunday evening – she's hardly home, to help me.'

I looked up quickly, just in time to catch a resentful glance from my tight-lipped mother.

Dear heaven! Now, what had I done? My needle slowed. Miss Ferguson knew how much washing, mending, ironing and cleaning, not to speak of child care, I managed to tuck into the time before and after work and during the weekends. She visited regularly and had seen me always busy. She now favoured me with a quick wry grin, and let Mother's complaints pass.

I looked at my flashing fingers as I darned. Broken nails and soot-ingrained cuticles, half-healed cuts and burns, all told of fires made, sooty saucepans scoured and food prepared. At work I hid my hands as much as possible.

'It is really time dear Helen was confirmed – I should have mentioned it before,' Miss Ferguson said persuasively. 'The confirmation lessons don't take very long – in fact, she may already know all that is required.'

So that was it. Well, I was quite happy to be confirmed if it pleased my Fairy Godmother, and thereby become a full member of the church.

'I suppose it is,' replied Mother. She flicked the ash of her cigarette into the tiny fire, which was almost lost in the huge, old-fashioned kitchen range. 'It is the time for the lessons – she really has to spend more time at home. I need her help.'

I let them continue to discuss the merits of Confirmation and the first Communion which would follow it, and went on darning and dreaming. Suddenly my heart jolted, when unexpectedly Miss Ferguson said, 'Of course, the dear child has never been to Confession. If she is to take the sacrament, she will need first to go to Confession. It would be a good idea, don't you think, if she got into the habit beforehand and went this week. Perhaps young Alan should think about it, too.'

I could feel myself going clammy all over. At that moment all the history books I had read, written almost entirely by Protestants, seemed to contribute to the sense of horror at anything which savoured of Catholicism – and Confession was surely a Catholic institution. In my nostrils there was suddenly the smoke and smell of the burning flesh of Protestant martyrs, made beloved by many a story; ordinary men and women, lords, priests, yokels, who had bravely faced being burned alive rather than acknowledge the Pope or the Mass – or confession to anyone but God.

I was weak on the theology of it, but I knew that Catholic Bloody Mary was the most hated Queen in British history, because she had tried to burn out of existence all signs of Protestantism. This unthinkable suggestion of Miss Ferguson's went against everything I had ever learned of my church. In a city riven down the middle by religion, it seemed incredible that a Protestant deaconess should ever mention Confession.

Needle poised, I burst into the conversation with a frightened squeak, a squeak of genuine horror. 'But we are Protestants. We say the General Confession during service. We make personal confessions only to God. I thought that was what being a Protestant was all about.'

Mother laughed, her delicate, superior, crushing laugh. 'Helen, we are High Anglicans. It is by accident that you have never been to Confession before. By chance, most of the places we have lived in have only low churches, so that when you were little you were taken to them.' She drew on her cigarette, and then added a little sharply, 'You seemed to have enjoyed going to a High Church recently.'

'In all the many months I stayed with Grandma I never went to Confession,' I protested. 'If she had gone, I am sure she would have taken me with her.'

Mother did not like being reminded of her mother-in-law, who had washed her hands of her shiftless son and would no longer have anything to do with us.

'Your grandmother was too old to walk further than the village church – and that church was low church.'

I pushed my fist into one of Brian's smelly socks and attacked another hole. My voice trembled, as I said flatly, 'Well, I'm not going.'

Miss Ferguson looked nonplussed, and her hands with their black cotton gloves fluttered helplessly.

Mother's heavily made-up face began to darken. 'Don't be ridiculous, Helen. It would do you good to go, to come face to face with your arrogance and bad temper. It might teach you to honour your parents, which would be a welcome change.'

Me? Confess? Tell some strange priest that there were times when I felt like murdering my mother? Times like this moment. Tell him that I had dreamed that I took all my clothes off in front of a man? I couldn't. I wouldn't. I could tell God himself these things in the course of the General Confession, because He had made me and probably understood His faulty work. But not a priest – not a man!

Much that I had let pass during my recent church-going suddenly fell into place. I had puzzled that the ministers of the church strode the streets in cassocks with black birettas on their heads, that servers assisted at the altar, that incense was used, the whole elaborate ritual. Now, the theatrical beauty of it, which had so impressed me, seemed suddenly to hide a basket of vipers.

Shivering but determined, I put down the darning into my lap and turned to Miss Ferguson. Her short-sighted eyes darted from Mother to me.

'Miss Ferguson, I couldn't do it. If I have to go to Confession, I might as well become a Catholic and do it properly. There wouldn't be any difference.'

Miss Ferguson found her voice and said rather hoarsely, 'There is a great difference, Helen. We do not accept the supremacy of the Pope. Our King is head of our church.'

Mother nodded agreement, her mouth pinched with her disapproval of me.

I felt as if I had been backed against a wall by a member of the Inquisition. I had never thought about the legitimacy of being allowed to worship as one pleases. I had no profound knowledge of my own faith. Most of my age group did not even attend church, though the majority, if asked, would say that they were either Protestant or Catholic – so great was the religious division in Liverpool.

To Liverpool Protestants, Catholics were people who lived in the worst slums because they did not know any better, and their greatest entertainment was attacking Protestant religious processions. They were not ordinary, kindly people at all.

I saw through Miss Ferguson's suggestion only the tortured faces of my own beloved martyrs. I ignored the fact that Protestants had, in their time, done their share of roasting hapless Catholics.

Miss Ferguson saw the need to reassure me, and she leaned forward and patted my knee. 'The first Confirmation classes will be held in a fortnight's time, my dear. Come along to the vestry. I am sure the good Father can explain to you much better than I can how good for the soul Confession is.'

'But – but . . . ,' I spluttered helplessly. 'Miss Ferguson, I can't – I just can't.'

The good Father! Not the Vicar. Childhood memories of gentle, vague scholars in clerical collars sipping tea in various drawing rooms made me want to rush back in time to them. I seemed to recollect that they only extolled the basic virtues. Where had they gone? I must have been asleep during the weeks I had been attending Miss Ferguson's church.

Mother was saying brightly that, since Miss Ferguson thought it wise, time would be found for my attendance at classes.

With her usual outward charm, she saw Miss Ferguson out of our grubby living room, into the narrow hall and finally out to the littered street. I knew very well that she would attend to me later in a very different fashion.

Though doubtless learned clerics were already discussing and challenging the concepts of hell and damnation and other long-held beliefs, eternal punishment for the heretic was a very real threat to a girl brought up by ignorant country servants and subsequently cut off from her contempories as I was. To defy one's parents for any reason was bad enough. To defy one's church was, in my opinion, likely to be much worse. As I contemplated Brian's tattered sock, I was shaking with fear of the spiritual forces which might be ranked against me. I wondered if I would be struck dead if I argued with the priests, actually raised my voice in a church building. And death was only the beginning of trouble for those cast out of the church. I might burn in hell for ever afterwards.

Nevertheless, quivering like a mouse before a cat, I determined on a last squeak.

Chapter two

I could remember Mother at the age of twenty-four, an elegant beauty with fashionable short black curls and large, pale blue eyes. Her fine legs were sheathed in the latest pure silk stockings, her skirts daringly short, so that a sudden flip of them would give a glimpse of ruffled silk garters trimmed with tiny roses or pearls, or French knickers heavy with lace. She attracted a great deal of attention from Father's war-battered friends, and Edith said she could get anything by merely fluttering her eyelashes. It did not work, however, when I tried fluttering my scant lashes, and I decided it must be something magical, known only to grown-ups.

The slightest argument or objection, the smallest frustration, would unleash her ungovernable temper, from which shell-shocked husband and servants would fly. I was terrified of her and would cling to Edith, seeking safety in her starched white lap. Edith always said comfortingly that she did not care a tinker's cuss about Mother's tempers; the job was handy for her. We lived conveniently close to the young farmer who was Edith's fiancé, and we frequently escaped to the warmth and laughter of his mother's farm-house kitchen. Alan, who was the child next to me in age, was also wheeled in his pram to the farm and got bounced merrily on many a rustic knee.

Now Mother was a middle-aged harridan, worn down by the illness she had suffered when my smallest brother, Edward, was born and by the privation we had all endured since Father's bankruptcy. Her figure was shapeless from eating too much white bread, her lovely legs horrible with varicose veins, hands ruined like mine, from washing, scrubbing, blackleading fireplaces, and lack of gloves. We rarely had hot water or soap, either for cleaning or washing ourselves, and face or hand creams were luxuries to look at through the chemist's window. All that remained of Mother's earlier self was a great charm of manner and a quick intelligence, when she felt like using either of them. Her scarifying temper had been further fed by her total unhappiness at her present state.

Like alcoholics, an improvement in my parents' lives could be brought about only by their facing their problems squarely and themselves determining on a new and careful path, in their case a financial path. But, like many alcoholics, they could not do it. So we all continued to suffer, despite the fact that five of us were at work.

Alan worked as an office boy in the city, and most of his small wages were handed back to him for tram fares, lunches and pocket money. Similarly, my pretty fifteen-year-old sister, Fiona, worked as a cashier in a butcher's shop. She earned the same amount as I did, but, unlike me, most of her wage was handed back to her for her expenses. Her clothes were bought for her, new, by paying for them by weekly instalments through a system of cheques. Companies issued cheques, commonly for five pounds, and with these one could buy clothing or household goods of one's choice at any store on the company's list. The clothing was often shoddy and expensive, but Fiona was at least as well dressed as any other girl travelling to work on the trams with her. I struggled to keep myself in clothes by buying them from the pawn-broker's bargain table.

Paying the cheque man was as much a worry to Liverpool housewives as finding the money to pay the rent, and it drained our income. We were per-manently hungry, frequently cold and not very clean. Cleanliness is expensive. Our landlord had freed us from one plague of slum living. He had had our house stoved, so that we were no longer verminous, and our relief from bug and lice bites was wonderful to us.

Brian and Tony, who came next to Fiona, had in-herited their parents' brains and they also had some of Mother's earlier vivacity and physical strength. Brian had won a scholarship from the church school to the Liverpool Institute, and I was very envious of him. Earlier, I had won a scholarship to the Liverpool City School of Art, but I had not been allowed to take it up. I had to stay at home to keep house.

Also at school was short, determined Avril, almost unnoticed unless she had a temper tantrum like Mother, and little Edward, beloved baby of the family, whom I had nursed along since infancy. Though Edward was not very strong, probably be-cause of the lack of adequate food in early childhood, his mind was clear and he had the ability to apply himself with great concentration to whatever he was doing. He could already read well, and Father hoped that both he and Tony would also win scholarships. Neither Mother nor Father gave any heed to Avril's possible abilities as a scholar. She was only a girl.

The only other members of the family to attend church were Brian and Tony, who for nearly three years had sung in the choir and had enjoyed a remuneration of a shilling and eightpence per month, which they were allowed to keep. Now they sometimes acted as acolytes. Nobody, as far as I knew, had pressed them to go to Confession. They were, however, the cleverest of passive resisters and even if pressed would probably have placidly failed to turn up for it. Brian's hazel eyes and Tony's calm blue-grey ones could look as blank as a factory wall, with an innocence and incomprehension of stare usually seen only in the subnormal. They were a pair of cheery scallywags, most unlikely to be faced with the inner qualms and soul-searching which always afflicted me.

I was dreadfully troubled when Mother ordered me to stop being such a fool, and to attend Confirmation classes. I made no reply, because I had long since learned not to do battle when I knew for certain that I could not win. For several days I fretted fearfully about what I should do.

'Them as don't obey goes straight to hell,' Edith had assured me, whenever I was being particularly perverse.

And there was Grandma's soft voice whispering, 'Good children go to Heaven, dear. Only the wicked burn in hell.'

And the Bible from which I had learned to read,

under Grandma's tuition, was full of the horrors of what happened to those who did not obey the will of God.

As I sorted files in the office, I tried to comfort myself. 'It doesn't really happen nowadays. It is an allegory.' But the fear in me was almost a primeval one; it stuck in the back of my mind and refused to be shifted.

Mother was obviously used to the idea of Confession. It must have been reinforced when she was a child, because she had been brought up in a convent, the only Protestant amid a sea of Catholics. It was waste of time to appeal to her.

Walking home through the April rain, I prayed to God to tell me what He wanted me to do, and got no immediate reply. Confused, afraid, with a mind filled with myths, I turned to the only other person I could think of who might advise me. I would ask Father.

Chapter three

To get a little time alone with Father would, I knew, be difficult. A big family in a tiny house has almost no privacy.

I pulled the string hanging inside the flapless letter-box, in order to let myself in. I had worked late and then gone straight to evening school and had not eaten since morning, but I paused for a moment in the doorway to watch some men playing ollies in the gutter. The little white balls skittered over the rough roadway, almost invisible in the light of the street lamps. These men used to say disparagingly about our family that we talked 'with ollies in t' mouth'. Refined Oxford accents were extremely rare in slums.

The smell of the house hit me as I went into the little hall, a smell of warm, damp, much used air, with strong overtones of the odour of vomit.

All the family was crowded into the small, back living room. Old-fashioned wooden shutters had been closed across the curtainless windows and secured by an iron bar. A small fire blazed bravely in the big, iron kitchen range, and by it Father was seated bolt upright in the solitary easy chair.

His usual yellowy complexion was flushed red, and he was pounding his delicate, almost feminine fist on the arm of the chair, as if to emphasise forcibly something he had already said.

As I paused by the door, he almost shouted, 'I will not tolerate such an abomination. It is disgusting beyond words. She must leave at once.'

He was answered by an unintelligible babble from the family.

I thought for an anxious second that he was talking about me. I lived in constant, gnawing fear that my parents would withdraw me from my job and make me stay at home again to keep house; they were quite capable of taking such a decision without any prior discussion with me and of handing in my resignation directly to my employer. I was still under twenty-one.

With some trepidation I eased my way through the half-open door and into the room itself. The children's upturned faces looked sickly in the light of the single, unshaded electric bulb, and Edward turned his heart-shaped face, pinched with fatigue, towards me. He said simply, 'Bed.'

Though he was nearly seven, he was no great weight and I picked him up, and said, 'Yes, love.' He and Brian were the only children I ever knew who asked to go to bed. It was as if their strength ran out suddenly. I smiled at him, and added, 'I'll put the kettle on to heat and help you wash your knees and neck as soon as it is hot.' I looked cautiously round him at the family.

The centre of attention was Fiona. She was standing in the middle of the group, facing Father, and her wide eyes with their enormous fringe of long lashes showed signs of tears. She was almost cringing, her toes turned slightly inward, her arms across her breast as if to protect herself.

She said in a watery voice, 'It's not that bad, Daddy. I didn't go. I wouldn't dream of it.'

Nobody took any notice of me, except Alan, who grinned at me as I stumbled over his feet, on my way to the kitchen with Edward. 'I think it's funny,' he said to Father.

There was some hot water in the kettle sitting on the greasy little gas stove, so I poured it into the washing-up bowl and commenced to wash Edward. I could hear Father's choked voice. He said furiously, 'It is *not* funny. It is horrible. At the least, it shows a total disrespect for the dead – at the worst, it is perversion. They ought to be put out of business.'

Mother was laboriously cutting her nails with our single pair of blunt scissors, letting the ends drop into the hearth, and she murmured, 'It makes me shudder.'

I paused in my preparations to wash Edward's dirty knees, and left him sitting on the kitchen table drying his face, while I went to the intervening door and asked, 'What's happened, Daddy?'

'Pack of sickening necrophiles!' Father exploded again, turning to me.

Brian and Tony were sitting at the table, elbows on open exercise books. I saw Tony's eyes light up. A beautiful new word to be learned, to be used incessantly for at least a week, while he turned it over in his mind and tried it in every possible way.

Mother greeted me with a worried, 'Hello, Helen. We'll explain it later. Put Avril and Edward to bed – it's getting late.' She turned to the students at the table who were obviously most intrigued by the

26

conversation. 'Hurry up, you two. Put your books away.'

'It's something about looking at dead people, Helen,' Edward whispered to me, as I returned to him, and rolled down his knee-high socks. His knees were very dirty and I scrubbed them with a piece of cotton cloth. There was no soap.

Avril had followed me out, and stood waiting for her turn to be washed. She said nothing, but her plain, round face beneath the straggling blonde hair was white, and I wondered if she were ill.

Edward struggled out of his woollen jersey and proffered a far from white neck to be washed. 'It's nasty,' he muttered.

Both children looked so bewildered and scared that I answered them with forced cheerfulness. 'It doesn't sound very respectful, I know. But I'm sure there's nothing to be afraid of. Dead people are just people who have shed an overcoat which has worn out. And the real people – their souls – have gone to Heaven. They are happy. It is only the people who get left behind who are unhappy – it's natural – they don't like being left.'

I tried to be soothing and matter-of-fact, while Avril perfunctorily washed her hands and face in the same pint of water.

Protesting crossly, Brian and Tony put their books together and heaved themselves between furniture and family towards the staircase and bed. Tony asked sulkily, 'How do you spell necrophile?' and was told angrily by Father not to be impudent.

I took the candle from the kitchen and eased Avril

and Edward along after the boys. Mother looked overwhelmed with fatigue, but she was not too tired to fire at Fiona, as I passed her, 'For goodness' sake, be quiet, girl.' Fiona sank down on an upturned paint can, which we used as a chair, and continued to whimper miserably.

Upstairs, I heard Avril and Edward say the small prayer which our nanny had taught me long ago, 'Gentle Jesus, meek and mild . . .' Then I tucked Avril into the bed she shared with Fiona and me, and put Edward into the one he shared with Brian and Tony, and left them shivering under the thin blankets to their individual nightmares.

Brian and Tony stumped grumpily round the room, pulling off their outer clothes and tossing them on to the bed rail. I put the candle down on an orange-box, which had been made into a dressing table by draping an old curtain over it, and told Brian to blow it out before he got into bed. 'Quietly, boys,' I pleaded. 'Let Edward go to sleep.' Then I ran downstairs again to the living room.

Alan had picked up a book and was flicking through it. Father and Mother were staring into the fire, Father rubbing his chin with quick, impatient motions. Fiona sat, her back against the wall, still crying. I was dreadfully hungry and quite apprehensive about what might have happened, but I went first to her and put my arm round her shoulders. She laid her head against my threadbare skirt. We never talked together – we had little in common except our sisterhood; yet we were often a comfort to each other.

'Daddy, what *has* happened?'

'She has to leave her job,' said Father, beating an impatient tattoo with his fingers on the arm of his chair. Mother nodded agreement. Alan put down his book and watched the scene with a look of morbid fascination, glancing expectantly from one to the other of us.

'Why?' I inquired, puzzled.

'She must,' Mother agreed, and then added crossly, 'It is not fit for a young girl – it is not fit for anyone to be there.'

Alan interjected with an unexpected chuckle, 'You could put it down to professional interest – after all, it's all meat.'

Mother was shocked. 'Alan! How could you say such a revolting thing?'

Alan grinned wickedly and folded his arms, as if enjoying the family's evident distress.

Father groped for words and finally said carefully, 'The butcher's shop in which Fiona is working is opposite an undertaker's. Sometimes the undertakers invite the butchers over to look at the corpses. I cannot believe that it is the undertaker himself who does this – I think it is some of his employees.'

Fiona lifted her face. 'It is, Daddy. They do it when he is out – and the butchers always wait until our boss has gone to market.'

'How awful!' I exclaimed. 'Imagine being stared at in your coffin by a pack of strangers. How morbid!' I looked down at Fiona's tousled head, and said to her, 'Perhaps you should look for another job.'

Fiona turned her face up towards me. She was so white that I thought she might faint. She said, 'They had a young girl there this morning – and she wasn't in her coffin – or even wrapped up. She was naked – and they were whispering and laughing afterwards about how they played with her. It sounded awful. So I was sick suddenly over the cash desk – and they laughed. After I had cleared up the mess, they sent me home early.'

Nausea began to overwhelm me. Vague tales I had heard, whispered amongst the beshawled women beside whom I had sat on front steps or in the park while watching the children play, began to surface in my mind and come together. I had always discounted their mutterings as rubbish. Now I realised that it was not rubbish. They had been disapproving about something which had really happened. I took big breaths to control my surging stomach. How could men be so vile?

'Heavens, I'm glad you told Daddy,' I muttered.

'I had to,' responded Fiona flatly. 'I was thinking about it again just before you came in – and I was sick over the floor.'

'Humph,' Mother almost grunted, 'I thought it was something else, but I was wrong, thank goodness.'

For a moment, I looked at her blankly and then remembered her bouts of morning sickness before every birth, and I said indignantly, 'Fi would never get herself into trouble. She's not that kind.' But a sudden, different fear for Fiona had been planted in my mind. Did she know anything about sex? I was still vague myself about the precise details of this mystery, but since I never expected to have a boy friend it did not matter in my case. It did matter for

Fiona. I knew that she was already meeting a local youth secretly and going to the cinema with him.

Father had been brooding during this exchange. Now he fumed, 'They should be reported.'

'Who to?' asked Mother.

'The police, of course.'

'Could the police do anything?'

'Oh, yes. It is a serious matter.'

'Oh, Daddy,' wailed Fiona, 'If you do tell the police there'll be such a rumpus in the shop. The men will say I'm a lying troublemaker, and the boss won't want to give me a reference.' She rubbed her wet eyes with the backs of her hands. 'The story will go all round the local shops, and then what will I do? With no reference, I won't stand a chance.'

She clung to me and I suddenly leaned limply against her. I was beginning to feel faint with hunger.

Chapter four

Fiona's situation was grave. When fifty youngsters were competing for even the most menial of jobs, lack of a good reference could be crippling.

'You can stay at home and keep house,' Mother said briskly. 'You spend all you earn – I never see much of it.'

'Oh, Mother, Fi only gets fifteen shillings a week, and she pays all her expenses – even buys some of her clothes,' I intervened vehemently.

Fiona's hands clutched convulsively against my hips. She, too, feared becoming the family's forgotten, unpaid maid-of-all-work.

Mother fumbled in her handbag for a cigarette and lit it from the fire with the aid of a newspaper spill. 'She would be more use at home,' she reiterated.

Father got up from his chair and moved restlessly up and down the narrow space between table and hearth which formed a passage between the front hall and back kitchen. He was very thin, and his grey tweed office suit with its shiny seat and elbows hung loosely on him. He looked haggard, as if this new problem was too much for him, and his face and prematurely bald skull shone pale yellow in the poor light. He took off his bent, gold-rimmed spectacles and rubbed eyes that were red-lidded and bloodshot.

'If I want to leave,' sobbed Fiona, 'I *have* to give a week's notice on pay day – that's Friday, and it's Friday night now. So it means I have to work almost another two weeks. And nobody is going to give a reference to a girl who leaves without notice – and how can I tell the boss the real reason I want to leave? It's too horrid!' She continued to dampen my skirt, as I held her.

Mother looked scornfully at her two daughters, her lips curled in disdain. 'Really, Fiona! All this fuss, when you could make yourself useful at home for once.' She turned to Father, and almost shouted, 'For goodness' sake, stop prowling.'

Father flung himself back into his chair, while Fiona cried, 'No.'

'She cannot mix with such dreadful people any more,' Father sounded off determinedly. 'What is the world coming to?'

'They leave me alone most of the time,' Fiona turned her puffy face towards Father. 'I sit in the cash desk and lock myself in. It has glass all round it. They tease me but they can't get in.' She moved uneasily against me. 'Only when I go to the loo sometimes . . .' Her voice trailed off.

Father started up. 'What?' he exclaimed. 'What happens then?'

'They chase after me and pinch my bottom,' she announced baldly.

'Oh, Lord!' Father was really shaken, as if he himself had never in his life pinched the bottoms of our maids.

Alan burst out laughing. 'That's better than being

33

whacked on your rear with a ruler, like I am.'

'Alan!' exclaimed Mother. 'What a lot of louts they must be.'

Father looked at his pretty daughter, speechless for a moment, and then said firmly, 'You will stay at home tomorrow, Fiona. Helen can phone from her office to say that you are not well. Then we will say later that you are not fit to go back. You can look for other work.'

'I'm not staying at home.' Fiona could be as wood-enly obstinate as Avril and me, but she never seemed to draw her parents' wrath as fully as we did. 'I just have to get through the next two weeks as best I can. Then I'll leave. After all, I've put up with them for nearly a year now.'

Father looked at her aghast. 'You mean all this has been going on for a year?'

'Not all the time.'

'How frequently?'

'You mean going to see the – the . . . ?'

'Yes.'

'Oh, they run over every time the undertaker has a nice looking one.'

'And have they been pinching you all that time, too?'

'No, Daddy, only just recently.'

'You must have encouraged them, Fiona.' This from Mother.

'Oh, no, Mummy. I suppose they notice me when they've nothing much to do. Anyway, how can a *derrière* encourage anybody?' she asked innocently.

This made Father smile, even in the middle of his

disquietude. Fiona's flawless figure, now burgeoning, would in years to come cause many a heart to throb and provide a good deal of temptation.

Father's voice was very gentle, as he looked at his younger daughter. 'I am sure you don't encourage them, my dear.' He smiled knowingly at Mother, who did not smile back.

Alan began to whistle softly to himself and moved restlessly against the table.

'If I had a sheet of the butcher's notepaper,' said Mother suddenly, her face brightening, 'paper with his heading on it, I could write an excellent reference for Fiona.'

'Mother!' I exclaimed, scandalised. 'That would be forgery.'

'A new employer might phone the butcher to check it,' suggested Alan.

'I don't think so,' replied Mother, ignoring my outburst. 'As a demonstrator going from shop to shop, I carry written references – I've heaps of them, because all my jobs are short-term ones. I don't think anybody has ever telephoned to check them.'

Fiona looked up quickly, and then mopped her eyes agitatedly with my hanky which I had handed to her – it was the only one I owned. 'Mummy! Could you do it? Really?'

Mother looked as pleased as a Cheshire cat. 'I don't see why not.'

'If I go to work tomorrow, I can get the paper easily. I have some in the cash desk.' She straightened up, sniffed and rubbed her nose hard with the hanky. 'I could start looking for a new job on Monday.'

It took Mother and Fiona some time to convince Father that it was the most sensible way out. But he was genuinely worried about his favourite daughter, and he finally gave in.

Alan thought it was a huge joke, and asked Mother if she could do anything about forging pound notes. I thought she would strike him, but instead she laughed.

Though it seemed to me to be wrong, that it might be better if Father had a quiet talk with the butcher himself, I did not want to start a family row, so I held my tongue.

On Saturday, Fiona went to work as usual and returned triumphantly with the required sheet of notepaper. Mother concocted an excellent letter for her, written in a round, illiterate hand quite unlike her usual beautiful penmanship. She ended it with a phrase popular amongst tradesmen, 'And oblige your obedient servant', followed by a flourishing signature.

Father often bought a *Liverpool Echo* on his way home from work. The day's copy was lying on his chair, so Fiona and I spread it out on the table and conned the Situations Vacant columns very carefully, though it was nearly midnight.

We found two advertisements for office girls, and Fiona begged Mother's penny pad of notepaper from her, took the cork out of the ink bottle and sat down at the table, pen poised. She looked up at me expectantly. To my dictation, she wrote in a round schoolgirl's scrawl letters of application to both companies.

Mother looked disparagingly at her handwriting.

'Really, Fiona, I should have thought you could write better than that.'

But Fiona could not, and never did. The teaching of handwriting in the elementary schools was so poor that few people seemed to leave with anything better than an ugly, irregular hand. Good, flowing handwriting, like the right accent, marked one's place in the social scale, and Fiona's laboured, round letters indicated a girl with a poor background, in a world which was very snobbish. Only Alan, who had been taught in preparatory school, wrote the same exquisite Italian hand which my mother did.

Fiona had a natural refinement and an endearing gentleness, without a hint of snobbery. She floated amongst all kinds of people without difficulty. Her letters, however, did not produce any replies, despite the fast postal service which we enjoyed, and Fiona became very depressed. Mother thankfully set her more and more household tasks each morning, and then borrowed her fares and lunch money, which meant that even if she obtained an interview with a firm, she would probably have to walk to it.

I encouraged her to keep on writing applications and, as my office was close to the *Liverpool Echo*'s office in Victoria Street, I dropped her replies each day into the newspaper's letter-box.

I had hoped to have a talk with Father on that busy Saturday, because both he and I finished work at one o'clock on Saturdays. Every time I thought about the coming Confirmation lessons, my stomach clenched with apprehension and I longed to unburden myself to somebody. But he had spent the afternoon at the public library, and after he had eaten his tea, he went immediately up to bed. He had had a heart attack when I was a little girl, and occasionally pain in his chest sent him hastily to lie down.

Chapter five

'Why can't I sign on at the Labour Exchange?' asked Fiona fretfully. 'They might have a job for me.' She was helping me to clear the breakfast dishes, and without make-up she looked tired and not very well.

Mother was putting on her lipstick in front of a piece of broken mirror wedged into the frame of the back kitchen window, and at this remark, she paused and said to Father, 'She might be entitled to Unemployment Insurance.'

'If she was, she has forfeited it by voluntarily leaving her position.' Father was running backwards and forwards between kitchen and livingroom like a demented hen. 'Where can my hat be? Have you seen it? I'll be late.' He called to Brian who was about to go out of the back door to school, 'Brian, wheel the bike round to the front door, there's a boy, while I find my hat.'

'I'll be late if I do,' complained Brian, his dark, heart-shaped face sulky, as he clapped his school cap on to his head.

'Oh, rubbish,' replied Father. 'Go and get it. And don't wear your cap in the house – you are not a workman.'

Brian slammed down his satchel on to the floor, flung his cap on top of it, and went to do as he was bidden.

'Why can't I?' reiterated Fiona, plaintively.

'Do you want to stand in a queue with a mass of unwashed, vulgar girls?' asked Mother. She quickly licked her forefinger and ran it over her eyebrows to remove the surplus face powder clinging to them. 'There is no point anyway. They would try to put you into domestic service. Do you want that?'

'No,' muttered Fiona dejectedly. Neither she nor I had ever considered going into domestic service. Even in my most deprived days, when I began to fear I would die from hunger, I had never considered this way out of my misery. Both of us remembered the servants in our own house when we were small. With the exception of their weekly half day off and on alternate Sundays, they were never free from six o'clock in the morning until eleven at night.

No. No domestic service for Fiona. Being at home was a shade better than that; at least one could have a good cry in the privy at the bottom of the back yard.

Father found his hat under the living room table, where the boys must have been using it as dressing-up material. He grabbed the bicycle from a fuming Brian at the front door, and pedalled creakily away to work.

'Never mind, Fi,' I comforted. 'What about writing to some of the big shops in the city – they like to employ under sixteens. I'll deliver the letters – or Alan can.'

Fiona's face lifted a trifle. 'Who should I write to?'

'Um – er, try Lewis's or Blackler's.'

'I'd love to work for Owen Owen's or Boots.'

I was hastily getting into my coat and hat. Given

good advice on how to improve her appearance, Fiona would have fitted well into these higher-class shops, but she was untidy and grubby, despite the fact that Mother bought her new clothes as often as possible. I said with caution, 'You could try them.' I picked up the letters that she had written the evening before. 'I'll put these into the *Echo* office for you.'

'Come on, Helen,' shouted Alan from the front door-step.

Mother told Fiona what to give the children for lunch and fled through the back door to catch her tram. Suddenly poor Fiona was left standing alone in the dirty, cluttered living room.

Some time back, I had been very ill and for two years had not been strong enough to walk to work. Recently because I felt better and, anyway, could no longer afford the tram fares, I had begun to walk again. Alan had always been provided with tram fares, but he started to accompany me. This long march to and from the city was hard on shoes. We both had pieces of cardboard poked into our footwear to help to fill up the holes in the soles. I had painful ingrowing corns on the bottoms of my feet from the exposure of the tender flesh to hard pavement. At times it was like walking on knives.

We always went along the side of the Anglican Cathedral. It was the last of the big Gothic edifices to be built in Europe, and clearly on the morning air one could hear the tiny taps of the stonemasons' hammers, as if a band of elves were hard at work. In pouring rain the great building looked like a huge red sandstone peak, and I loved looking at it, though I had never yet plucked up enough courage to enter it – I feared I was too shabby. Alan did not share my cat-like interest in new territory, so when I suggested that we go into it together, he shrugged and asked, 'Whatever for?'

Along Rodney Street, with its charming Georgian frontages, its trim white front doors and gleaming brass plates, he made me stop several times. It was a street of medical specialists, whose cars parked in the street reflected their owners' status. Alan would pause to touch reverently a polished door handle or a new shiny mascot sitting proudly on a bonnet, and would point out to me the merits of the various makes.

Sometimes he would talk enthusiastically about the cricket matches which he played in the park. He was always the hero batting steadily against the opposing team's wicked bowlers.

Occasionally, he would ruefully rub his bruised bottom and mutter maledictions against the ruthless bookkeeper under whom he worked as an office boy. Older men were heavy-handed with their apprentices. They believed in knocking a young man into shape. They had never heard of bruised egos, and a bruised bottom was just one of the hazards of being young. Boys of fourteen found themselves a small minority amid older men and they learned their trade and how to behave, whether they liked it or not. Perhaps that is why in those days there was less vandalism and less theft. In big, soulless places like the docks, however, theft was a fine art.

I rarely talked to Alan about my own affairs. I was, after all, a stand-in mother to him. I listened. It was unusual for me to talk very much to anyone except my friend, Sylvia Poole. I never seemed to be able to stop talking to her. Ever charitable, Sylvia always said she learned a great deal from me. She certainly received a great number of lectures on British and French history.

Neither Alan nor I mentioned the necrophiles amongst whom poor Fiona had found herself working. To me it was another sickening facet of human behaviour to be shunned, condemned and put out of my mind. Alan had made a joke of it, and I wondered if he really thought it was funny. It must have been in his mind, because he said suddenly, as we hurried down fashionable Bold Street, 'You know, Fi is very dumb. She was lucky she didn't get raped in that place.'

'She's not so stupid, really,' I replied. 'She had enough sense to lock herself into the cash desk – like a doll in a glass case. She's so pretty. Too nice to be pushed around.'

I caught my breath as a stab of pain went down the side of my stomach. A familiar dull ache spread down my back.

My step faltered, and Alan paused to ask, 'Something the matter?'

'No. Nothing much. Just a little spasm. It will go.' I clutched one arm across my waist, to try to contain a second wave of pain.

'You look awfully white.'

'No. It will go,' I reassured him, and moved forward again, pressed by the crowd behind me hastening to work.

Alan must have been aware that each month I was seized by terrible, clawing pain lasting some eight to twelve hours. It was impossible to hide it, because I would faint from time to time. Yet I could not bring myself to tell him what the trouble was. Our National Health Insurance doctor assured me that it would disappear when I married, which was not much comfort to a born spinster. He never examined me. I took aspirin in large quantities. Mother bought me ground ginger to take in hot water and, if the pain struck while I was at home, I had the use of Edward's hot water bottle to hug. Nothing helped much. I wondered how I would ever crawl through the day's work. I had no sanitary towel with me to use, and no money to buy one. We used bits of old cotton cloth which we washed over and over again.

I did not consider returning home. People who missed too many days of work tended to be dismissed at the first excuse, and I had lost a lot of days through illness already. If I fainted in the office it would be all right. Women frequently fainted from overwork, lack of food and all kinds of untreated illnesses.

I felt a stab of another kind as we moved slowly onward. The pin holding up my panties had opened and scratched me, and in seconds they slid down my legs and lay round my ankles. Alan giggled, as did one or two passers-by.

Proud as hell, I felt so humiliated that I started to cry quietly, as I stepped out of them. It was not the loss of the panties that bothered me; it was their grey raggedness. They were tattered beyond repair, elasticless, patched on patches, in a world where a

44

good pair could be bought for sixpence – and they were already stained. I did not know how to endure the look of disgust on the face of one nicely dressed woman who stepped round me. I wanted to scream at her that it was not my fault that I was not clean.

'Pick them up quick and put them in your bag,' said Alan, a grin on his face.

I did so, hastily cramming them down into the old-fashioned handbag, and we moved on quickly. Alan produced a hanky and I surreptitiously wiped my eyes. The pain was coming in low level, steady waves.

'Thanks,' I murmured, as I handed it back to him. The handkerchief was grey from poor washing. Sometimes it seemed as if we lived in a world which was made up entirely of shades of grey and black.

We came to the corner of Whitechapel and Church Street. Here our ways parted.

'All right?' Alan asked.

I hesitated for a second, wondering if he could lend me three-halfpence for a tram ride home. Fear of piling up more absences than my employer would tolerate made me say, 'Yes, thanks. 'Bye.'

I shuffled up to the office. What was I going to do? I would have to ask one of the girls for help. Would they again think me to be a disgusting object, lacking even basic commonsense to provide myself with ordinary sanitary requirements?

Filled with consternation, beside myself with pain, I climbed the six flights of stone steps to the cloak-room on the top floor.

Chapter six

There was no one in the cloakroom and it gave me the opportunity to attend to myself as best I could. I replaced the errant panties, pinning them firmly this time.

With eyes closed in pain, I washed my hands. The water belched forth from the tap, gloriously hot, and I thought how heavenly it would be to lie in a bath full of it, to ease the cramping pain. And the soap – how lovely it smelled.

There was a quick tap-tap of high heels on the linoleum on the landing. The door burst open and in flew the Head Cashier. She was a small woman, swathed in a green overall, a rigid disciplinarian. Today, her forbidding expression boded ill for anyone she met. I hastily busied myself drying my hands.

She ignored my good morning. 'Where are the girls?' she demanded. 'Everybody is late.'

I trembled. Without exception, all the younger employees dreaded this ferocious lady. Her Assistant was never known to open her mouth, and her Junior Clerk was so frequently reduced to tears that her eyes seemed permanently lachrymose and her nose was red from much mopping.

'Well?'

I started to say that I was going downstairs to work

immediately, when such a sharp, tearing pain hit me that I clutched the white roller towel and let out a moan more like the shriek of a woman in childbirth.

'Good gracious, girl! Whatever's the matter?' Her usual bitter expression vanished.

My senses were leaving me, and I whispered, 'It's my period.'

She was much shorter than me, and elderly, but she said firmly, 'Pull yourself together. Now, put your arm round my shoulder. I'll help you into the Committee Room. You can sit down there.'

Eyes clenched shut, mouth open as I continued to groan and gasp, I thankfully put my arm round her shoulder and she supported me into the adjoining room. She dumped me on to a wooden chair and then put three other chairs together, and assisted me to lie down on them. The wood of the curved seats was not comfortable, but it was better than having to stand.

A couple of books from the bookcase were put under my head. She arranged me on my side with knees tucked up in a foetal position. Then she stood back, hands on hips, and surveyed me.

I could not control the deep, primeval groans that burst from me, as the pain surged in ever greater waves. Tears would come later, when the agony was gone and I was left exhausted.

'Poor girl,' she exclaimed suddenly. 'It's worse than childbirth.'

Childbirth was something I hardly understood at that time, but much later in life I found that indeed she was correct.

'I'll get the office girl to make some strong tea,' she

promised, 'and I'll send up some aspirins.' The scarifying Department Head had vanished completely and a very understanding woman had emerged. She did not waste time telling me to be brave or to stop the noise I was making. 'You lie here and try to relax yourself – it might help.'

I whimpered, 'Thank you – but aspirins don't help much.'

'They should if you take enough. We'll try what four tablets will do.'

I curled myself up tighter, as another roll of pain went through me. 'Mr Ellis . . . ?' Mr Ellis was the head of my department, a man of few words, usually very tart ones.

'I'll deal with him,' she promised, and whisked out of the room.

It seemed a very long time before the door opened slowly and the office girl slid in with a tray of tea things. The girl was a replacement for my friend, Sylvia Poole, who had left to take training as a chiropodist. I wished frantically that Sylvia was with me. She was so sensible. I was very cold and was lying on my back, knees up, swaying them from side to side, unable to find easement, and threatening to fall off my perilous perch. As each peak of pain was reached, I would put my clenched fist against my mouth to muffle a shriek, and then moan, a noise which came from the depth of my being and had nothing to do with will.

The tea tray was put on another chair drawn close to me, and the frightened little girl, a mouse, aged fourteen, fumbled in the pocket of her blue overall.

'She said I was to give you these.' She handed me four aspirins from one pocket and then, very shyly, a sanitary towel from the other pocket. 'She said I was to help you while you put it on.'

That meant I had to get on to my feet and make a trip to the cloakroom. I lay with eyes closed, wondering if I could do it.

'She said to tell you to take big breaths,' announced the girl, watching me pop-eyed, as if I were something in a cage.

'Ask Miriam Enns to come and help me,' I winced. Miriam was a stenographer, one of three who worked in a small office next to the Committee Room. She was in her late twenties and had been very kind to me. A dedicated Communist, she tended to attempt to recruit quite ruthlessly, so I had begun to avoid her, since I was not politically minded. I was too engrossed in trying to stay alive, to sidestep Mother's terrible tempers, to educate myself, to be a good employee. To survive was all I asked of life.

Miriam came running. 'Whatever happened?' she asked. Her reddish hair drooped smoothly round a pixie face. She had a big mouth which could curve into a smile so sweet that one could hardly believe in the strong Party Worker lurking within. But she had the physical strength I needed very badly.

The moment she saw my contorted face, she understood. I had taken refuge before in her little office on several occasions when I had been struck like this while at work.

Miriam looked down at the tea tray and sent the

office girl away. 'O.K., love. Have the tea first. Have you got any aspirin?'

I opened my clenched hand, to show the four tablets. She raised her eyebrows. 'That's a lot.'

I took a large breath, as instructed. 'The Cashier said – take four,' I gasped.

'Well, I suppose she'd know.' The Cashier was never referred to by name, only as She or The Cashier. I called her Madam when I had to speak to her.

'Oh, Miriam!' I nearly screamed.

'You'll be all right, dear.' She poured the tea and held it to my quivering lips, while I swallowed the aspirins. Then she sat by me and chafed my hands and talked about seeing a doctor.

'I did, Miriam, and he just laughed – said I'd be all right when I married.'

'The stupid fool,' she exploded. 'Consult someone privately.'

'Miriam, I don't have money for things like that.'

She was referring to doctors who practised outside the National Health system. I was registered with a National Health doctor and it was difficult to change one's physician under this system. I felt I was lucky to have one doctor on whom to call, never mind anyone else. In suggesting a private physician, Miriam was, for once, allowing her middle-class instincts to outweigh her socialistic convictions.

I choked down the aspirin, and then we staggered to the cloakroom like a pair of drunks. Miriam kept one foot against the door, so that no one could enter, while she helped me wash myself.

Back in the Committee Room, she rearranged the

chairs and I lay down again, while she ran downstairs to take dictation from one of the senior staff.

The pain did not go, and I longed for home. I suppose that the Charity could not afford a taxi to send me home – they were very short of funds – and I certainly could not go on the tram. The Society did own a car, but it was in use all day taking workers to visit clients in distress.

For a while, I continued to lie on the chairs, but then removed myself to the linoleum floor, where I could move more easily. The floor was very cold, but it was flat. Nowhere in the building, which housed some twenty-five women, if one included the employees of a tea company on the ground floor, was there a couch or easy chair for staff use. There was no place where one could eat a packed lunch, except for the minute kitchen adjacent to the Committee Room. Truly, the tailor's child is the worst clad, and we lacked facilities which were increasingly being provided by thoughtful employers.

Half way through the morning, the Cashier sent the office girl in with more tea and two more aspirins. Thirty grains of aspirin in little over an hour and a half did have some effect. The top edge of the waves of pain was less sharp. I lay with eyes crunched shut and wondered if the pain was a judgment on me for refusing to go to Confession.

I could not eat the slice of bread and margarine I had brought for lunch, but I drank eagerly a cup of coffee which Miriam poured for me from her own thermos flask. Miss Short, the Head Typist, kindly provided two more aspirins.

Forty grains of aspirin. I was not sure how much one could take without poisoning oneself. I knew that a hundred aspirins would cause death – it was a popular form of suicide amongst women. Mother took as many as twenty in a day. She had no physical pain to assuage, but she said they soothed her nerves; suffering from nerves was a socially acceptable ailment – Liverpool women often referred to 'Me poor nairves'. Mother also smoked twenty to thirty cigarettes a day, as did Father.

The pain finally lessened, and when the other clerks returned from their lunch break, I went downstairs and reported shyly to Mr Ellis.

'Oh, aye,' he said absently, when I said I was feeling better. 'Take t' index cards and sort them – there's a lot.'

I sat down at the corner of a table which was my place in the crowded room, and spent the rest of the afternoon sorting the little white cards into alphabetical order and then standing to file them in long wooden drawers. The aspirin and exhaustion combined to make me feel sleepy, and sometimes I felt as if I was floating on a sea of distant pain.

When the office girl brought in the afternoon tea, she also carried a message from the busy Cashier, who worked in the next room. How was I? Would I like some more aspirin? She spread out her grubby little hand to show two tablets. I swallowed them gratefully with the tea.

The secretary to the Presence – the Presence was my name for my austere employer – thundered away on her typewriter at the other end of the table, but on seeing me take the aspirin, she paused to inquire what the trouble was. Through tightly clenched teeth, I told her I had a monthly pain. She nodded sympathetically and renewed her thunder. The other clerks running about with piles of files in their arms had no time to stop to ask after my well-being.

It was the longest of afternoons. The noise and vibration of the typewriter in front of me, the sound of the buzzers and bells of the old-fashioned telephone switchboard behind me, the filing clerks pushing behind my chair as they ran to and fro, made the close-packed room almost unbearable. Clients crept in and out, to see the Presence in her office which led off the room I was in. Chairs were dragged across the floor for them to sit on and even that vibration went through me and made me hurt all the more.

It did come to an end, however, like everything else in life, and I had to admit to Mr Ellis that I had not completed my day's work.

'Humph, then we shall have to work faster tomorrow, shan't we?'

I agreed humbly, and put the remaining cards in the table drawer.

In the cloakroom, I met Miriam struggling quickly into her overcoat. She stopped to inquire how I was.

'Better,' I said. With my eyelids drooping with fatigue, I turned to hang up my overall.

'You usually walk home, don't you?'

'Yes.'

She buttoned up her coat and picked up her handbag. 'You'll take the tram tonight?'

'No.'

53

'For Heaven's sake, why not?'

I forced myself to look at her and said dully but honestly, 'I don't have any money.'

'Oh, child! Why didn't you say so before? I'll lend you twopence – you can pay me on payday.' She rustled round in her handbag and proffered the coins. I took them gratefully. I had been troubled all the afternoon wondering whether I would manage the long climb up the hill to home.

Liverpool trams swayed like a ship in a storm and I began to feel nauseated. I was glad when the vehicle came to a stop at the Rialto Cinema and I could descend, while its motor hummed like a hive full of angry bees as if to say it could not wait to let me off.

As I stood on the corner of Upper Parliament Street waiting for the traffic to clear so that I could cross the road, my eyes began to dim and I knew that I would probably faint. But where to take refuge on such a busy corner, with its lounging groups of unemployed men gossiping idly?

Facing me stood the Rialto Cinema and dance hall. It had a wide pillared entrance and a sweeping curve of steps. I could lean against one of the pillars, I thought, under the supervising eye of the girl in the cash desk. If I actually passed out, she would undoubtedly call for help for me. Two or three people obviously waiting for friends to join them were already standing on the steps. People would think I was waiting for a boy friend to take me to the cinema.

The Commissionaire glanced at me. He was a shrimp of a man in a gilt-trimmed uniform too big for him. I leaned against the wall of the entrance at the furthest point from him, and closed my eyes.

'You O.K., love?'

It was a man's voice. Wearily I opened my eyes. A man neatly dressed in a light raincoat, tightly belted, and a trilby hat rakishly tipped over one eye was standing in front of me smoking a cigarette.

I knew him by sight. He seemed to spend a lot of time hanging around that corner. Once, while I was buying groceries, he had come into the shop to purchase some cigarettes, and after he left the shopkeeper called him a damned pimp when speaking to another woman customer. 'Got three girls, he has,' she had said.

He had, however, the pleasant smile and easy manner of so many smart alecks making a living in the streets, and I answered, with a sob in my voice, that I was quite all right, thank you. I winced and turned my face away. He did not leave me. Instead, his voice quite compassionate, he asked, 'Like a cigarette?'

The steps of the cinema looked wavy when I again opened my eyes, and my legs threatened to give way. I glanced at the proffered case. It was finely worked silver.

'No, thanks, I don't smoke,' I responded.

'Try one of these,' he urged, poking at some small brown cigarettes in one side of the case. 'They're great for headaches – make you feel on top of the world.'

I sighed. 'It's all right, thanks very much. I'll be O.K. in a second or two. I live quite near.'

He helped himself to an ordinary white-papered

cigarette and threw the stub of the old one into the street. He tapped the new one on his thumb nail before putting it into his mouth, then closed the beautiful cigarette case and stowed it in an inner pocket. He produced a matching petrol lighter, lit the cigarette and exhaled leisurely through his nose. 'Yeah,' he said. 'I know you. Seen you often.'

At this I stared, pain forgotten. Then I realised that if I knew him by sight, it was very likely that he knew me as a local inhabitant. I smiled wearily and straightened myself up. His cigarette had not lit properly and he flicked his lighter on again. The tiny flame showed for a moment a coarse but not unpleasant face, with calculating black eyes. I felt I was being weighed up.

'What do you do, like – work?'

'I'm a clerk.'

He nodded, and I said goodnight, and slowly walked the short distance home.

It is strange to think that if, in the acuteness of my pain, I had accepted the Indian hemp which he had offered me and it had created sufficient euphoria to dull it, I would have wanted to obtain it again. Undoubtedly, he would have approached me again, anyway, in the hope of my becoming hooked. Then he would have promised me clothes, food and a flat if I would work for him, and I would have slowly sunk into the dregs of Liverpool.

But I knew from reading and from one or two cases I had seen at work what hashish could do to people, and almost instinctively I had refused.

Chapter seven

The back living room seemed packed with people all talking at the tops of their voices. The family had long since finished its tea and, normally, I would have quickly eaten whatever had been kept hot for me in the oven which lay alongside the fire. Then I would have cleared the dishes and washed them up and put Avril and Edward to bed before going to night school. Tonight I had no strength left.

Mother, in a soiled house dress, was sitting in Father's easy chair, reading the *Echo*, her bare feet on a wooden chair – to rest her veins, as she always said.

'Hello, dear,' she greeted me amiably, glancing over the newspaper. Then she put the paper quickly down on her lap. 'Are you ill?'

Sometimes I was more afraid of Mother when she was being considerate than when she was quarrelsome. I answered carefully, using the polite expression for what had happened to me. 'I was unwell.'

'How are you now?'

'A bit better, thanks. I won't go to night school tonight – I'll hand my German essay in on Wednesday.'

I took out of my handbag the crumpled confectioner's paper bag which held the uneaten lunch of bread and margarine. 'I'll take this for tomorrow's lunch,' I added as I laid it on the table.

'Gosh,' exclaimed Fiona, 'You must be hungry.' She went quickly to the oven and lifted out a plate, using the hem of her skirt to protect her fingers from the heat.

I smiled at her gratefully, as she put the meal down in front of me, a tablespoonful of stewed minced beef, a potato and the inevitable pile of frizzled up cabbage.

'Mother bought some jam tarts and we kept one for you. Here it is.' She pushed towards me a second plate with a little tartlet in a paper case sitting on it.

Mother was watching me, as I sat down, and I asked if she could spare two aspirins.

'Of course,' she said, and got up to find them in her handbag. 'Would you like some hot ginger?'

Even in pain, this horrible thick concoction of ground ginger mixed with hot water was something to be avoided, so I refused it with suitable expressions of gratitude for her kind thought.

'Eat your tea and go to bed,' she advised, and returned to her perusal of the paper.

Edward put his tousled brown head out from under the table where he and Tony and Brian were playing cards. 'You can use my hottie if you've got a tummy-ache,' he offered. He loved lending his hot water bottle to other members of the family. Some kind soul, responding to the begging letters Mother wrote quite regularly, had sent it with a parcel of clothes. Since it was unpawnable, Edward had always had his bed warmed by it.

I laughed for the first time that day and thanked him, as he ducked back underneath the table. The healthy noise of play in the room was a godsend to me. So often my parents fought or the children squabbled and howled. Amity was something to be cherished.

Avril was playing by herself at her favourite game of dressing our latest alley cat in an old baby shawl and putting it to bed in a box. She was talking softly to the patient animal.

Mother had dropped the aspirins by my plate, and Fiona brought some weak tea, made by pouring fresh water over the old leaves in the pot. Mother leaned forward and poured a cup out for herself and for me. Absently, she popped two aspirins into her own mouth and swallowed them.

Father and Alan were seated on old paint cans, trying to rewind the thread neatly round the handle of a time-worn cricket bat that one of Alan's colleagues had given him. Both had nodded to me when I came in; now they started to argue as to the best way to secure the thread.

'Snap!' came a delighted shout from Tony under the table. 'I've won. I've won!'

'No, you haven't,' responded Brian indignantly. 'Something's wrong. All the Kings have been played before. There must be an extra one in the pack.' He had a most retentive memory, but neither Edward nor Tony would accept his contention. An altercation broke out, as they scrambled round in the tiny space, while they checked the incredibly battered pack of cards with which they always played.

I ate my tartlet, while Mother leaned down from her chair and shouted at them. The raised voices vibrated through my wracked body. The tartlet did nothing to assuage my hunger, and I considered eating the lunch which I had brought back home. But I was not sure that there was enough bread in the house to provide me with lunch the following day, so I left it wrapped up in its old margarine papers.

I went upstairs and took a piece of cloth from a pile at the back of a dusty, built-in shelf in the bedroom. These rags had been accumulated from bits of sheeting and garments bought from the second-hand shop and torn into squares. Mother, Fiona and I used the same collection for our periods, washing them again and again. We were always nervous of running out of them.

The pain was rapidly easing now, and I went downstairs again, through the living room where a fight between the boys seemed about to break out, through the little back kitchen with its clutter of unwashed dishes, into the tiny backyard, lined with brick, to the lavatory by the far wall.

We were lucky to have a flush lavatory to ourselves. There was still a number of courts in Liverpool, surrounded on all sides by houses containing a family in each room, where all the inhabitants shared two lavatories set in the middle of the court.

Ours was a dank, cold outhouse, and its pipes or its tank froze every winter, causing bursts which sometimes took our aristocratic landlord weeks to repair. Copies of the *Liverpool Echo* lay on the long wooden seat, for use instead of toilet paper.

When I returned, Fiona had filled the hot water bottle for me and I thankfully took it and went up to bed, leaving the family to cope as best they could with the work I usually did.

The bed I shared with Fiona and Avril now boasted a bottom sheet and three pillows with pillow cases. The linen was grey with poor washing with insufficient soap, and sometimes with no soap or hot water; but it indicated an improvement over earlier days when I had slept on a wad of newspaper covering a door set on bricks, with an old overcoat to keep me warm.

I crawled on to the lumpy, smelly mattress and drew the two thin blankets up to my chin. I placed the hot water bottle carefully on my aching stomach; it was so hot that it seemed as if it might skin me. The rest of me was very cold despite the comparative mildness of the weather, and my knee joints and ankles hurt quite sharply whenever I moved.

Then the tears pent-up during the day exploded and I cried bitterly until I could cry no more. I cried from weakness, from cold, from hunger, from despair that life would never get any better, a holocaust of loneliness, of frustration, which seemed to pick up brief pictures of the pain-filled day and whirl them maddeningly in my head. Despite my fear of burning in hell if I did not go to Confession, I began to pray passionately to be allowed to die.

But God evidently had other things in mind for me, because I continued to survive.

Chapter eight

I slept so deeply that I did not hear Avril or Fiona get into bed, but when Father's alarm clock clamoured its warning of six o'clock, I was automatically out of bed and on my feet in a flash, anxious to get into the kitchen before the others, in order to wash myself in private.

Father trailed down the stairs ahead of me dressed in the tattered remains of a camel-hair dressing gown his sister had given him for his sixteenth birthday – the only garment apart from what he had been wearing that he had brought from our old home. He went straight to the kitchen range to rake out the cinders and build a new fire, while I put a kettle of water on the gas stove for his shaving and for Mother's early morning cup of tea.

I filled the washing-up basin with cold water from the tap, stripped off and quickly washed myself from head to foot. Mostly I had to make do with water and a cotton rag – occasionally there was soap for my face. When the kettle boiled, I padded across the tiles, naked, filled a cup and handed it to Father through a crack in the door. He then shaved, without a mirror, in the living room, using an old-fashioned cut-throat razor and a stump of shaving soap. As soon as I had some clothes on, he would enter the kitchen and make Mother's tea, occasionally holding the razor dripping with soapsuds in his left hand, half his face still lathered, the other half shining clean. The early morning offering of tea was one of the few things Mother appreciated about Father. She always thanked him and drank the weak, scalding liquid slowly, while shouting instructions about clothes or breakfast to various members of the family.

Fiona was usually the main target of her criticism in the mornings. In all her younger days Fiona never managed to prepare her clothes or lunch for the following day. The fact that the boys took it for granted that their clothes, books and lunches would be prepared for them and that they could, therefore, be considered equally inefficient was lost upon Mother; girls were capable of looking after themselves; boys were not.

If the fire that Father had made did not catch, I tried again with it, while he washed in the kitchen. First, old copies of the *Echo* were crumbled up to make a base, then a small pyramid of wood chips, bought from the chandler in neat wire-bound bundles, was built, upon which small coals were laid. A match was set to the paper and, if the wind was in the right direction, the chimney would draw the flames upwards and the fire would catch. In addition to coal, we burned vegetable peelings wrapped in newspaper, worn out shoes, anything that would burn was burned. I had long since given up collecting rubbish from the streets to keep the fire going, because I felt we should be able to afford enough coal to give us a little fire, morning and evening. Nevertheless, despite five of us having work, the coal cellar was often empty, particularly in the autumn and spring, when Mother felt we should be able to manage without heating. At such times we kept the windows tightly closed and the damp, badly constructed house acquired an icy stuffiness, an unwholesome exhalation of nine half-washed bodies.

This morning, Fiona, wandering about in her grubby nightgown, kindly laid the breakfast table for me and fed Edward and Avril.

Alan had recently very proudly begun to shave with a safety razor. He was rather slow at it, because his face was a dreadful mass of acne spots, great pustules painful enough in themselves without an added nick from the razor. Sometimes the pimples came up on the back of his neck and the pressure of a stiff collar band aggravated them, until they became big open sores that took a long time to heal.

While Alan shaved, Brian and Tony washed themselves. They pushed and shoved against each other, as each tried to insert a finger into the tap, so that they were doused by the resultant spray. The stone tiles of the kitchen were often running with water by the time they had finished.

Avril and Edward, having been perfunctorily washed in warm water before they went to bed, got a quick wipe around their mouths with a damp cloth and a flick of the comb from either Mother or me.

Except for Mother and me, everybody ate a small dish of cornflakes with milk, followed by a slice of bread and margarine, sometimes with a little marmalade. Weak tea was the drink of the whole family.

In the interests of economy, Mother and I ate a piece of bread and margarine only.

Quite frequently, Mother did not work in the mornings, so often the children came home at lunchtime to a hot meal, usually of minced meat or of eggs, with potatoes and cabbage or carrots. When she did work before noon, a meal of bread and margarine and cold meats was prepared by Mother or me and left on the table for them, and we tried to provide something hot for them at teatime.

Father and Alan took a lunch with them of bread, margarine and cheese. Since I made up the lunches, I always made mine last, and there never seemed to be any way in which I could divide the small amount of Canadian red cheese so that I could have some without leaving them short. The severe illness I had suffered two years earlier had left me very apathetic about myself; it was enough for me if I could crawl through the day without incurring either Mother's or Mr Ellis's wrath and perhaps get a kind word from my dedicated night school teachers.

Mother was a demonstrator. She took short contracts with department stores who wanted to launch new kitchen gadgets, and she stood in the store and showed people how to use them. Occasionally, she did door-to-door selling for vacuum cleaner companies, family photographers, Christmas card publishers or sweet firms. When doing outside work, she wore an all enveloping leather coat which she had bought second hand. This protected her from Liverpool's damp, cold wind, and, despite its bulk, she still managed to look elegant in a faded way. She had a lovely carriage and an authoritative voice with a pure Oxford accent. She was a very good saleswoman.

Her supervisor in a vacuum cleaner company, who once called at the house, said admiringly, 'She could steal your front door key off you and sell it you back before you knew it had gone.'

Father received this doubtful praise in stiff silence, while his guest threw a cigarette stub into the hearth and smoothed his curled moustache.

I do not know what Mother thought of some of the men with whom she worked, but it is doubtful if their crassness bothered her much. She was so sure of herself, so certain of her social superiority despite our current circumstances, that she was to a degree armoured against them.

Father was different. He was abject in his failure and very easily hurt. His public school training, followed almost immediately by war service in Russia during the Revolution, had given him little preparation for a world which had changed completely by the time he came home. He might have survived better had the Depression – and a large family – not added to his difficulties. Like many soldiers returning from the First World War he was emotionally and physically drained by its unremitted horrors; there was little real strength left; and I could guess at the cold flame of hatred in his heart, when faced with a runt of a salesman, who was probably doing rather better than he was as a City clerk.

Mother came downstairs with the coarse white teacup in her hand, and paused when she saw me in the hall to ask if I felt better. I said I did. How could I complain of overwhelming fatigue to someone who looked like a haggard ghost herself?

As we stepped out of the house into a beautiful, rain-washed morning, glad to be away from a fetid, crowded home, Alan offered to pay my tram fare to work. He was shy about referring to my aches and pains of the previous day, but he was well accustomed to their occurrence.

'No, dear,' I said. 'I shall be all right. In fact, the exercise is good for me.' And I marched beside him down the street as if I had not a care in the world. I could not take his pocket money; but I loved him for the sheer kindness of the offer, and our conversation held more than its usual friendly warmth.

'The man from the furniture shop came last night – after you'd gone to bed,' he informed me, as we paused to look in the window of the bicycle shop at the corner of Bold Street; and he sighed over black enamelled frames and racing handlebars.

'Oh, dear!' I exclaimed. 'What now?'

'Threatening to take it away again.'

'Haven't they been paid lately?'

'Suppose not,' he replied gloomily.

'Oh, blow. It's such an appalling waste, Alan. Mummy and Daddy make the weekly payments for a while. Then the stuff is repossessed – but we still have to pay for it – it doesn't get us off the hook. It's so stupid. Really, they're absolutely crazy.'

'Humph.'

He was not very interested. He never used our front sitting room. His friends did not come to visit

– he always met them on the cricket or football field or in the park, where they would sometimes kick a tennis ball about in an impromptu game.

I was very interested, because payments for the furniture represented a heavy drain on our income. It was money that could have been spent on food and coal. Mother always hankered after some semblance of prosperity, and this was the third room full of sitting room furniture she had bought on the hire purchase system, while ignoring our frantic need for bedding and beds, coal, hot water and food. It was easy to obtain furniture for a very small down payment and weekly payments, laden with interest. Failure to pay resulted in prompt repossession of the furniture, without releasing the buyer from his financial commitment. So the loss could be a heavy one, particularly if one had nearly completed the payments. The three separate firms we had to pay or face being sold up entirely by the bailiff, swallowed enough money to have fed us well. Twice the sitting room had been emptied by phlegmatic furniture removers, well used to pushing their way into the houses of debtors. Now it seemed that it might happen again.

Chapter nine

The great port of Liverpool lies on a series of hills rising from the waterfront, and each day I climbed the long slopes from the city centre, on my way home. I passed concert halls, hospitals, surprisingly finely built Edwardian public houses, rows of little shops and tasteful Victorian houses, some of which were falling into decay. Every so often there was a newsagent's and tobacconist's shop, and I depended upon the hastily chalked newspaper headlines displayed on boards outside their shops to alert me to the big news of the day. They currently dealt with the crises of the Spanish war, about which Miriam frequently held forth passionately in the office. She foretold quite accurately that it was but a dress rehearsal for a much bigger conflict. They also announced the forthcoming coronation of George VI and his plump little Duchess, Elizabeth. Some of these shops were decorating their windows with souvenirs, coronation mugs, flags and brooches. A number of defiant people still wore pins and brooches with the insignia of Edward VIII, to show they thought that he should be the king, despite his intention of marrying an American divorcée.

I never saw a billboard that dealt with Liverpool's fearful slums, some of the worst in the country, nor the hunger in them. Occasionally an increase in the number of unemployed was mentioned, and a great march by workless men who walked all the way to London got some attention. The slums with their suffering inhabitants had always been part of the Liverpool scene; they were not interesting.

Trudging homeward through pouring, slashing rain, I had no particular desire to arrive. Too often more problems, more worries awaited me.

This evening, to my astonishment, there was good news. Fiona had received a letter asking her to go the following afternoon for an interview with a magazine-distributing agency. She was as agitated as an aspen in the wind, and while I ate my tea, she discussed with Mother what she should wear, as if she had a wardrobe full of clothes instead of a single blouse, a skirt and two dresses which were almost outgrown.

Mother was being most cooperative. She offered to lend her a hat which had recently been refurbished with the aid of a bright yellow feather and a new ribbon into what was known as a Robin Hood style. Mother knew that when a shorthand student had paid me a few days earlier I had bought a pair of rayon stockings, so she lent her those as well, despite my protests that the pair I had on could not be mended any more; they were laddered beyond redemption.

After returning from night school, I spent a couple of hours fuming as I oversewed ladders and darned heels, and then lengthened one of Fiona's dresses for her. It was after midnight before the hem was finally hand-stitched and pressed, but Fiona who had never learned to sew was touchingly grateful.

There were times when I wished that Grandma had not taught me how to use a needle. When I was a child I used to stay with her for long periods of the year in her house on the other side of the Mersey river, but she no longer had anything to do with us, because Father had quarrelled bitterly with his family.

Mother had learned from nuns who brought her up how to do fine embroidery for copes and altar cloths, but she was not adept at other sewing. She sometimes darned socks if I was too busy to do them or if I had, in a rage at the pressure put upon me, temporarily struck work. Nine people in near rags produced a lot of sewing, by necessity to be done by hand. My eyes were always tired from short hours of sleep, constant reading for night school and from my day-time work, all done with the aid of spectacles long since outgrown and in need of replacement. Quite often the work was done by candlelight, because we did not have pennies to put into the electric and gas meters.

Apart from Fiona's letter, there was a letter for me to give me pleasure. To improve my German I had a pen-friend. He was the son of a schoolmaster and lived, as far as I could judge from the map on the wall at night school, about forty miles from Munich. The idea was that I should write to him in German and he would write to me in English, so that we would both benefit. However, he soon fell into the habit of writing in German. This had for me one fortunate result. Because Mother did not know German, she gave up opening and reading my letters before allowing me to have them, something which I had always bitterly resented.

In early April, he had sent me some violets, carefully pressed, from his garden. His letters had taken a slightly sentimental turn, and he wanted a photograph of me. It was very thrilling, though Hitler's stern limitations on foreign travel and my poverty made it almost certain that we should never be able to visit each other. As a young boy, he had already visited England on an exchange plan, and that was how I originally met him.

When this pen-friendship first commenced, I had had the utmost difficulty in finding money for stamps out of the shilling a week allowance I had squeezed out of my parents. Miriam in the office had willingly contributed sheets of typing paper and some envelopes, and I usually wrote to him in my lunch hours, using the office kitchen counter as a desk because it was clean. I had a tiny pocket German dictionary which my German teacher had given to me, and as my grasp of the language improved I wrote with its aid ever lengthening letters.

Too shy and ashamed to tell him of the grim poverty into which we had fallen, of the filth, hunger and vermin which were my daily companions, I wrote as if we were still living in our old home and I was attending the local high school – a private school which took girls of all ages. I described the house, the servants and our social life. My grandmother and her home, shared with two aunts and a cousin, were also sources for description of English life. As time went on, I wrote of my hopes of becoming a qualified social worker in Liverpool, and he responded by saying that he would become a schoolmaster, like his father. We had lively discussions on books which we had both read and on religion, but he soon discovered that if we touched on politics or if I sent newspaper cuttings, the letters were not received, indicating censorship of both inward and outward mail, presumably in Germany.

I had also acquired a girl pen-friend in Stettin, through an offer, in the correspondence column of a Sunday newspaper, to put children in touch with each other. Judging from her photograph, she was exceedingly pretty, an ash blonde, and was the daughter of some small government official. She was impatient of my bad German, which was very good for me, but she gave me such long and involved explanations of German grammar and idioms that I sometimes did not understand all she said. She was one of a class of students who had been encouraged by their teacher to seek English pen-friends, and both sides seemed to get quite a lot of fun out of it. What neither side knew was that we had been drawn into a minor spy network, and this was to cause me no little distress when the war began.

Ursel, aged fifteen, and I were blissfully ignorant of all this and discussed the scary prospect of her father arranging a marriage for her, when she was passionately in love with a boy who travelled on the same bus as she did each day. When she was not correcting my grammar, she wrote pages on every detail of the young man. They had never got beyond smiling at each other – but for nearly a year her hopes ran high. At the age of sixteen, a marriage *was* arranged for her by her father, to the minister of her church, a man of forty, and the last letter I received from her a few days before the war broke out was from a young girl broken-hearted and pregnant. It would have moved even a bored censor. Poor Ursel – and the war with its repression of the clergy and its ruinous fighting was yet to come.

Chapter ten

Fiona went for her interview. Father provided her with threepence for the tram fares to and from the city, and she returned glowing with excitement.

'I think I've got it,' she said, as she took off the Robin Hood hat with its bright yellow feather and handed it back to Mother. 'They said they'd let me know – they want to see one or two other girls before deciding.'

She did not return my stockings, but she was so relieved and happy that I did not want to spoil things for her. I did not tell her that the phrase 'We'll let you know' was the stock dismissal of an unsuccessful candidate. She would learn the sad facts of job-hunting in Liverpool by experience. She had been fortunate in finding her first job, because few girls would want to work in a butcher's or a fishmonger's shop, and she was probably by far the smartest fourteen-year-old to apply.

I went on sweeping the living room's tiled floor and then worked my way over the small piece of coconut matting in the middle, briskly brushing the dust and debris towards the hearth.

'What kind of work is it?' Mother inquired. She was seated at the table, writing pad and bottle of ink before her, and she did not look up from her composing of a begging letter. She still occasionally wrote to perfect strangers asking for financial help, and quite frequently received compassionate replies enclosing a welcome pound or two.

Fiona sat down on the easy chair and clasped her hands in front of her. She replied eagerly, 'They would teach me to use a thing called an addressograph. It makes the labels to put on the magazines they send out. They've got hundreds and hundreds of magazines, lovely ladies' magazines and story ones – everything. They send them out to subscribers. They've got so many that they even have to have a van to take them to the post office.'

'Are there many on the staff?'

'No. Two gentlemen saw me – and an old lady who does the books. I don't think there was anyone else.'

'What's the pay?' asked Alan.

'Twelve shillings and sixpence a week at first, and then in two months' time – if I get quick at managing the machine – they'll give me fifteen shillings. Isn't it great?'

Alan looked amazed. 'Holy Cain! You lucky thing! I'm only getting seven and sixpence – and Helen's been working nearly three years – and she's only getting twelve and sixpence.'

I was actually receiving fifteen shillings, but I dared not say so. The precious half-a-crown difference was what had paid my fares during the time I had not been strong enough to walk to and from work, and now it sometimes bought me a bowl of soup in Woolworth's cafeteria when there was nothing left at home for me to take for lunch. My shorthand student, when I had one, paid me enough to

76

cover my pair of rayon stockings every other week and the bits and pieces of clothing from the pawn-broker's bargain table.

Fiona laughed, looking suddenly like Mother when she was young and full of vivacity. 'I'm so excited.'

'It's lovely,' I agreed heartily. 'Lift up your feet, people.' They all automatically raised their feet off the floor, while I swept neatly in and out of the chair legs. Like an army, they put their feet down on the floor again in perfect unison when I reached the hearth and picked up the pile of dust between my hands. I threw it into the fire and there was an immediate outcry from the others at the horrid odour of burning hair, as it hit the hot coals.

Father had been sitting silently on a wooden chair at the opposite end of the table from Mother, while he drank a cup of tea left over from our meal. He rested his head on his hand and, except for the red acne rash across his nose and cheeks, his face was pale. Now he said, 'I'm very glad about the job, Fiona. What happened this morning about the furniture?'

All the joy was immediately wiped off Fiona's face. She said sadly, 'They came and took it – like they did before, Daddy. They just pushed past me and walked in when I opened the door.'

'Pack of bullies,' said Father angrily. 'And to think that we've already paid two-thirds of it. They might have waited.'

Personally, I thought the furniture company had shown the patience of Job waiting for their money at different times. But I knew enough to keep my mouth

77

shut. I put the broom away and went upstairs to get my account books, so that I could do my book-keeping homework.

When I returned, Mother was saying, 'We could let that room. Nobody is going to let us have more furniture on the never-never plan for a while.' I smiled at her use of Liverpool's name for the hire purchase system, which never, never seemed to get paid off.

'Well, it might help to pay the furniture instalments,' said Father wearily. 'Some business girl who has her own furniture, perhaps?'

I sat down by him and opened my ledgers. 'She'd have to pass through this room and the kitchen every time she wanted to get water or go to the lavatory,' I pointed out.

'Oh, you always look on the black side of things,' Mother grumbled. 'I don't suppose such a girl would be home very much.' She folded up her letter and put it into the envelope. 'I'll advertise it in the news-agent's window. I wonder what rent I could get?'

'A small room rents for about seven shillings a week,' I told her, as I carefully made entries in my collection of books.

'How do you know?' Mother was cross. She licked the envelope and rubbed her hand impatiently across the back of it to seal it.

'Well, Mummy, I see details of dozens of people's incomes and expenses at the office. The first thing an interviewer does is to fill out a form about the client with all kinds of details.'

'I think that's about right,' Father agreed. 'I see

plenty of them, too. With no bathroom in the house, we can't charge much.'

'I'll try for ten shillings,' Mother said firmly. 'After all, this is a very respectable house.'

She wrote an advertisement on the back of an envelope and immediately went out to see the newsagent, who would, for twopence, exhibit it for a week in a glass case hung on his door.

Fiona had had an early tea before going for her interview and now announced that she was going to see a girl friend. Alan drifted off to play cricket with the other boys in the street. I should have gone to call Avril and Edward to come in because it was their bedtime, but for the moment I was alone with Father. He had picked up his library book and was looking for his place in it. I laid down my pen.

'Daddy, could I ask you something?'

'Yes, dear.' He closed his book again and peered at me through his spectacles. I noticed that the gold frame was bent, so that one eye was not looking through the middle of the lens, and it gave a curiously lopsided appearance to his face.

I reminded him of Miss Ferguson's desire to see me confirmed, and that she expected me to go to Confession before taking my first Communion.

'I've been so worried, Daddy. What is it all about? I never dreamed of having to go to Confession. I thought old King Henry VIII and Queen Elizabeth did away with such things in the Church of England? I'm so frightened, Daddy – is it wrong to refuse to go?'

He chuckled. 'Good Lord, no. There's nothing to be frightened about. The Church of England allows considerable latitude within its ranks – you must know that.' He sighed heavily. 'Both your Mother and I were brought up as High Anglicans – in fact, you probably know that your mother was actually brought up by Roman Catholic nuns, despite her being a Protestant.'

'Hm,' I agreed.

'But then there was the war. And, you know, it was difficult after that to believe in anything. We rarely went to church after that, except to get you children christened.'

'You go to the cenotaph every November 11th, no matter what,' I reminded him with a little smile.

'Yes, I do. But that's just so that my old friends – my dead friends, wherever they are – know that I remember them, that I have never forgotten them.' His voice was suddenly shaky. 'There were only three survivors, you know, from my old regiment – the three of us who volunteered for the Russian campaign.'

I could not bear the stricken look on his face, and I selfishly recalled him to my own predicament by asking, 'Must I go to a High Anglican church, Daddy? Couldn't I be confirmed somewhere else? Edith always took us to the village church – and they had very plain services, I remember – and neither you nor Mother said anything.'

Again he sighed, and then he looked up at me with a little smile. 'As far as I'm concerned, dear, you can go to any Protestant church you like, if it gives you comfort. I know you are trying to live a good life – and church will help to keep you out of mischief.'

Mischief was the last thing I was ever likely to get into, and I laughed, a laugh tinged with great relief.

'Really? Would it be all right? Could you talk to Mother about it?'

'Of course. Your Mother won't mind, and I expect Miss Ferguson will get over it; she will probably be offended at first, though, because you always seem to have been a protégée of hers.'

'She's been a fairy godmother – and I'm truly sorry if she becomes angry about it, but even for her I can't face Confession.' I picked up my pen and chewed the end of it, and then said passionately, 'I'd burn first.'

Father laughed. 'You're a real Protestant – but I'm glad for you that you seem to have a clear belief, God bless you.'

Such a weight rolled off my shoulders. The smell of sulphur and brimstone, the smell of hell, which had haunted me uneasily for days, rolled away.

I jumped up from my chair and leaned over to kiss his bald pate. 'Thank you, Daddy.'

He caught my hand and squeezed it, while he looked up at me earnestly. 'Religion is a private thing – remember that. If you can find a path to God which suits you, take it. I wish I could, but I am not able to feel anything any more – as I said, it was the war.'

I put my arm round his shoulders and sought in my mind for comforting words. 'Perhaps you will change as time goes on, and the memory of the war becomes less.'

He nodded. 'Perhaps.' But he never did.

I was the one who changed. Starting from Father's

unexpectedly wise counsel, I began to look at others' religions with a wider and more inquiring mind, as I moved about Liverpool and met people of all beliefs and all nationalities. Edith was fond of remarking that the gentry had too much book learning and not enough real learning, and it took a while for me to remedy this imbalance.

The ice between Father and me had been broken. Older now, I was more able to forgive and understand his weakness and in reaching out for his aid when I was so afraid, I think I had restored to him in some small part a sense of being wanted, being needed for more than the wages he brought in.

Whether his talk with me had alerted him to the possible code of behaviour of his sons, I do not know. He began, however, to check on where they went in their spare time and what they did. He made them all promise to tell Mother or me their destination whenever they went out. Nobody thought of Fiona and Avril. The boys all had lively, inventive minds and were fairly well mannered. They tended to draw friends to them, whose parents were glad to have them play in their houses, where they were under supervision. The boys also frequently played together, and this helped to keep them out of bad company.

Father's new interest in his children was wonderful to me. One of the most scaring things in childhood is the lack of an older person to turn to, to depend on for guidance and advice. Now, in a diffident, irregular way he was beginning to make his presence felt in the family, as if the trauma of the war and his financial ruin was beginning to be sloughed off. Though, in fearsome battles, Mother still shouted him down, he persisted quietly, using a strong sense of humour which I had not realised he possessed.

Chapter eleven

Two women came on separate occasions to view our empty front room. One of them was an elderly widow and the other a shop girl in crumpled black – black was the uniform of work in those days. The lack of a bathroom and an indoor lavatory made them both turn it down with supercilious sniffs.

A few days later, a young Irish labourer, cap in hand, came to see it.

'I'm sorry I am not prepared to let the room to a man,' Mother said, beginning to close the front door on him.

'It's not for meself only,' pleaded the youth. 'It's me wife and me baby.'

It is doubtful if anyone, except the poorest slum landlord, would have considered such a tenant. Labouring in Liverpool meant casual work at rock bottom wages – and a consequent difficulty in paying the rent. A baby meant noise and a lot of washing to be hung out. And Irish people did not have much of a name for cleanliness.

I saw Mother hesitate. The careworn white face with its red-rimmed, pleading eyes must have touched some chord in her – perhaps she remembered when she had canvassed from door to door, trying to find a landlord who would accept seven children. 'Is your wife with you now?'

'She's waitin' at t' corner.'

'Ask her to come. She'd better see it, too.'

Joyfully, he turned and bawled up the street, 'Mary, coom 'ere.'

A plump, cheery woman wearing a black shawl, with a young baby wrapped in the front of it, came panting up to the doorstep. Her rosy face, and thick light brown curls bobbing round her shoulders, reminded me of Edith, our nanny. They both had the same country-fresh look. Her expression was one of sudden glowing hope.

Fiona and I were longing to see the baby, which seemed very small, and when we had all trooped into the bleak front room, from which even the curtains had been removed by the hire purchase company, Mother asked if we might see it. Its tiny puckered face under a clean, frilled bonnet was tenderly admired by all of us, as it placidly slept.

' 'E's only six weeks,' his mother announced proudly as she wrapped the shawl back over him.

Mother stood in the middle of the unvarnished square of wooden floor, where the carpet had lain, and explained the disadvantages of the room. The young couple were irrepressible.

'Och, I can keep a couple o' buckets o' water in t' room. And Pat will be gone to work before most of yez is up.'

'We're all away during the day,' Mother informed her, 'except for a little while when the children come home to lunch.'

'To be sure,' responded Mary, with a wide, sweet smile, 'I can do me washing and cooking while you're all away.'

'You can hang the washing out to dry in the back yard,' said Mother. 'Come and see.'

We all went out to view the tiny, sooty yard with its lavatory near the alley door.

'We could keep our coal in the corner here,' suggested Pat. 'I could roof it over with a bit of a tin roof, like.'

'Where are you living now?' asked Mother, as we returned to the house and entered our living room.

'We're living with me Mam,' replied Pat. 'It's too hard on Mary, though. Me Mam isn't an easy woman, I know. When we was in Dublin we was living with her Mam, and that was all right, wasn't it, Mary?'

Mary nodded agreement, and sighed. We all understood. In Liverpool–Irish families, daughters frequently brought their husbands to live in their family. Husbands escaped from their mothers-in-law by going to work and then in the evening going down to the local pub for a drink. The young wife, however, had recourse to no such escape route if faced with her husband's mother – and the result was battles so bitter that they sometimes spilled out into the street and caused a street fight, a welcome entertainment to the onlookers, but unpleasant for the combatants.

As we showed the young couple round, I had become more and more resentful of Mother. I believed that she was raising the couple's hopes, without having any intention of giving them the room. Now, to my astonishment, a bargain was struck; a rent of ten shillings a week, plus one shilling for electricity, payable in advance.

'If you want to use the gas stove in the back kitchen, you will have to put your own pennies into the gas meter,' Mother instructed them. It seemed fair, but in practice we were more likely to benefit from gas left over by them than they were from us, because we always seemed to run out of gas and money before we had finished cooking. We had to try to complete the job on whatever bit of fire we might have at the time.

'We'll bring our gear over on Saturday afternoon,' Pat said. They both thanked Mother gaily, and through the undraped window we watched them laughing and talking together, as they hurried up the street.

Mother was the strangest person, I thought. There were layers of her character of which one caught only a momentary glimpse. Our tiny house would now have twelve people living in it, all using the same outside lavatory and the same cold water tap. The inconvenience of people trailing through our crowded living room and kitchen at all times of the day and night would be indescribable. Our frequent bitter family rows would be heard clearly by these strangers, the details in due course to be gossiped to the neighbours. The clash of uneducated Roman Catholic Irish with upper class Protestants was something I dreaded. Yet, watching Mother's drawn face, I was sure she had taken the family in out of compassion. Admittedly the rent was more than half the rent of the entire house, but nothing could compensate for the overcrowding and loss of any small privacy we had.

Mother and I went back to the living room and

were met by a barrage of questions from the children, who had watched in silence the small procession to and from the back yard.

'Yes, they are coming to live with us,' Mother told them. 'You will have to be quiet so as not to wake the baby – and be polite to them.'

Alan raised his eyebrows and made a rueful expression at me, while Fiona just shrugged her shoulders. Father was out having a drink with a young colleague with whom he had recently become friendly. Fortified by several glasses of beer, he received the news optimistically when he came home. Perhaps he felt, like me, that a week of such an arrangement would see the end of it.

Chapter twelve

To my surprise, Mother accepted my diffident announcement that I would prefer to be confirmed by another church, with only a fretful, 'What am I going to say to Miss Ferguson? Really! Don't you have any consideration?'

I was much too shy to go to see Miss Ferguson myself, and I do not know what explanation Mother gave her. I never saw her again, though I did hear her once when Mother sent me to borrow a shilling from her, with the plea that we had nothing for breakfast – which was true. Mother had already coerced out of me the few pennies I had, so feeling very sick at heart I had trudged to her flat, through dark streets, where the gas lamps gleamed dully through a sea mist.

The lady with whom she lived answered the door. She did not know me, and when I inquired for Miss Ferguson I was told that she was having a bath. Fearing Mother's scathing tongue if I returned without the shilling, I nervously whispered the reason for my visit. She left me standing in front of the open door while she went to consult the bather. There was a mumble of voices in the little apartment; then clearly I heard Miss Ferguson say, 'Better give it to her. Get it out of my bag – it's on the dressing table. I'm tired of that woman – she never pays back.'

I wanted to turn and run. Miss Ferguson probably lived on a pittance, unless she had private means. The stranger was, however, hastening down the hall towards me, at the same time feeling inside a small black handbag. When she reached the door, she unsmilingly handed me a silver coin and shut the door on my muttered 'thank you very much'.

I stood looking at the offending woodwork and wanted to throw the coin at it. Mother had lost a good friend for the sake of a shilling – which she could have easily saved had she not smoked.

Mother received the money with triumphant relief, and sent Avril out to buy bread and margarine, milk and cornflakes.

So kind Miss Ferguson vanished, as far as I was concerned, into a dish of cornflakes. Fairy godmothers do tend to depart when their work is done.

When Pat and Mary and the baby arrived, it was clear that they regarded Mother as a fairy godmother. They brought their bits of furniture on a handcart; it took two journeys. An iron bed frame was put together in the room, with much bumping and rattling of metal slats which had to be woven across the base. A wool-packed mattress tied with string was banged down on it, making the slats again vibrate in tuneful protest. A wash-stand with a marble top, innumerable galvanised metal buckets, a pile of enamelled wash basins with a few dishes laid inside the top one, two chairs and a small table, some iron saucepans, a tea chest of assorted garments and blankets with a chamber pot perched on top, a fine old handmade cradle on rockers, all were piled into the room. There was only one small cupboard, which had once held a gas meter, and I wondered how everything would fit in.

Mary pinned up over the small bay window a pair of dusty looking lace curtains. They did not give much privacy when the light was on, but they looked fairly tidy from the outside. It was only from occasional glimpses through the curtains when I passed in the evening that I was aware of the muddle of their lives. Nobody to my knowledge entered the room.

The young couple evidently decided that to make the situation bearable for both sides, they should be as invisible as possible. We were barely aware of Pat, except as a shadow going out to work through the front door as Father and I came downstairs each morning. He spent half of Sunday in bed with his wife, judging by the giggles we heard and the pinging bed slats. Mary once said primly, 'Men must have their rest on Sundays.'

To use the lavatory in the yard, they went out the front way, walked past three houses and then down a side alley which led into our back alley, and came back in through the yard door to the privy. They rarely pulled the chain, but at least they did not come through our living quarters. Nobody commented on this long tour they had to make so often, and I doubt if the family appreciated their consideration.

While we were out, Mary cooked huge quantities of stew in an enamelled wash bowl on the gas stove. I sometimes saw her hurry through our living room with this vast amount of steaming meat and vegetables, smelling so savoury that I was envious. I think she cooked enough at one time to last two or three days and that she heated portions of it on the fire in their room. I once caught a glimpse of the room's interior when I opened the door for her when she was thus laden. Three big pails of coal and three of water were ranged against a wall. A pile of washing was flung into a corner. The baby's cradle stood close to the fire. The wash-stand was littered with utensils for cooking, the mantelpiece laden with anonymous bottles and jars. The table and chairs were, I knew, set in the bay window – I had seen them as I passed – and the rumpled bed was against the hall wall, behind the door. The wooden floor was bare and grimy, but it had been swept. A thick effluvia of human living rolled out, a mix of stew, onions, baby's faeces, sweat, urine, and steam from the washing drying on a string hung from the mantelpiece. It added itself to the neglected grubbiness of our part of the house. I hastily shut the door after Mary's, 'Thanks, luv.'

After a few days, we discovered that Mary had found an old built-in wash boiler in a corner of the coal cellar. Rather than use a similar one in the corner of our kitchen, she had carried water downstairs and had boiled her washing in it by making a fire in the tiny grate underneath. She did all her washing down there amid the clammy smell of coal dust and cats. Then she hung the clothes to drip in the back yard, before bringing them to finish drying in her room. She was very resourceful.

I probably saw more of her than the others did, because I was almost invariably the last person to go to bed; I often did my night school studying after everyone else had gone up to bed. She would slip apologetically through the room several times, carrying buckets of coal and water or a pile of washing from the back yard. She also emptied buckets of dirty water down the kitchen sink.

Occasionally, while I was studying by candlelight because we could not afford a penny for electricity – candles cost a halfpenny – she would hasten in with a penny because they also were plunged into darkness. I always continued with my candle, because I felt it would be unfair to switch on the light and help use up their pennyworth.

On Saturday night, Pat, with a shy grin on his face, would knock on our living room door and hand to whoever opened it, eleven shillings. They had no rent book and never asked for a receipt. Their trust was moving.

Because of the poor quality of the building, any raised voices could be heard in the next room, and they must have suffered from the continual squabbling of the children and the bitter, screaming rows between my parents.

Sometimes they themselves quarrelled. In their case, it was not always a verbal spate. There were the sounds of screams, scuffles and thumps, while the baby howled untended. Fortunately, perhaps, our children found it funny rather than frightening. Most of the time, the baby was quiet, cosied against his mother's ample breasts or rocked in his warm cradle by her foot on the rocker, while she knitted.

Occasionally, Mary would stop in her late night promenade to ask me what I was doing. She smelled strongly of milk and perspiration, but she had a glowing life about her, an eager effervescence that I wished was mine. She was endlessly curious about us and boundless in her praise of Mother. I began to see Mother in a slightly better light. 'To be sure, she's a great lady,' Mary would remark at times, and I wished I could feel the same about her.

One night, I had been wrestling with a difficult task which my English master had set me. I was to read a book of essays by William Hazlitt and comment on it. I was very tired and could not concentrate and was asking myself why I bothered, since it would make no difference to my marks, when Mary, carrying a pile of dirty washing, entered without knocking.

She paused, smiled and asked, as an opening gambit, 'How are yer, luv?'

Relieved to be temporarily delivered from Hazlitt, I put down my pen and pushed the cork into the ink bottle.

'Not bad, Mary. How are you?'

She looked at me hard. 'You bin cryin'?' she inquired solicitously.

I had cried, after everyone had gone to bed, letting the tears drop on to my books. Mother had paused on her way to bed, and had asked me with a hint of contemptuous curiosity what I was going to wear for my forthcoming Confirmation. Her attitude was cold, as if she were poking idly at a half-dead beetle on the floor.

I had never seen a Confirmation, and it was with a sense of shock that I received the information that I would be expected to appear in a white dress and veil – a fact which was confirmed by the head of the church's Sunday school, the following week, when after the evening service she announced to the congregation that veils would be loaned by the church.

In a world which still judged people by what they wore – a moment's consideration of a person's dress would establish his position socially – I was in a difficult dilemma. To buy odd garments to cover me was hard enough; to buy a dress for a single occasion was impossible. I would, presumably, need white stockings and shoes as well, which would never be worn again.

Mother had not offered any answer to her query, so there was not much hope of help from her. I said, tight-lipped, that I did not know what to do, but I would think about it, and opened my books and got on with my homework as best I could with a mind in a nervous flutter. Life never seemed to get any better and this additional problem made me cry with dumb despair.

'We all have a little cry sometime or other, Mary.' I tried to smile.

'Oh, aye,' she agreed. 'I like a good cry meself sometimes. Relieves you, like.'

I nodded and piled up my books. I would have another try at Hazlitt tomorrow during my lunch hour.

Mary shifted the washing round in her arms. It reeked.

'What's to do?' she persisted.

I sighed. 'Well, Mary.' She was always Mary,

95

never Mrs O'Neill, to all of us. It marked the difference in class. 'Well, Mary, I'm going to be confirmed.' And I went on to explain the problem of the dress.

Mary was thrilled. Confirmation was a great event, she burbled, though in her opinion it should have taken place when I was seven. 'Och, you'd look like an angel, in white,' she assured me, looking my beanpole figure up and down. 'Surely your Mam will get you a frock?'

'She can't afford it,' I defended Mother. 'And I don't have a penny,' I added frankly.

Mary clicked her tongue. '*My* Mam got me one – and for sure we didn't have much money. It's a very special occasion.' She glanced down at the washing in her arms. 'Look, luv, just let me take me washing down. We got to think how to do this.'

She tripped down the stone steps to dump the washing in the copper. When she came up she had a coal smudge on her apron and was dusting it off impatiently. She stopped in front of me, and announced almost defiantly, 'If you can't get a dress any other way, I'll lend you me wedding dress.'

'Oh, Mary!' The offer was so kind, but Mary's figure was rotund and anything of hers would have hung on me. Yet her dress must have been almost a sacred relic to her amid her present hard circumstances. I hesitated.

She must have read my mind. 'It's proper nice – and it'll fit near enough,' she said. 'I was real thin when I was married.' She looked down at her enormous bosom and giggled. 'Marriage agrees with me. I'll have a word with your Mam.'

When I came home the next evening, Mother greeted me with such enthusiasm that I was frightened. But, according to Avril, Mary – dear Mary – had indeed been talking to her, pointing out that other than my marriage or my funeral, Confirmation was the greatest day of my life, even if it was to be performed by a Protestant bishop.

Before I even got my coat off, Mother was saying, 'Just come and look.'

Laid on a chair, with a sheet of newspaper under it so that it was kept clean, was an open dressmaker's box with a large pile of white tissue paper in it. Mother carefully parted the tissue, took out a dried sprig of orange blossom and laid it on the table, while she gushed, 'Isn't that sweet? It's from her wedding bouquet.' Then she carefully lifted out a pile of lace and shook it. It was a charming, long sleeved white dress.

I gaped as I looked at its shimmering whiteness, its absolute purity of line. 'Mother! It's lovely. It's perfect. They must have spent a fortune on it.'

Mother laughed. 'Well, you should know by now that a working class wedding is a great event. And they spend money on them.'

Mother carefully folded the dress back into its tissue. As she lifted the package and handed it to me, a few grains of lavender fell from it. I bent over the box's contents and sniffed. It smelled like Grandma's sheets and dresses, with a lovely perfume of fresh lavender.

'Mummy's going to buy you some white shoes and stockings – and a petticoat,' interjected Fiona. 'Aren't

97

you, Mummy.' She said it firmly, as if to reinforce the decision.

'Of course,' said Mother, without blinking an eyelid. Fiona winked at me. Mary, she told me afterwards, had swept Mother along on such a flood of excitement that Mother had said she would apply to the finance company for a cheque for a pound, to cover the purchase of these accessories.

To persuade Mother to buy me anything was little short of a miracle and, with the box still in my arms, I knocked on Mary's door, and went in to thank her. She blushed as I kissed her. Then heaved her baby round on her lap to offer it her breast, and muttered, 'It's nothing, luv. Nothin' at all.'

So, for the first time I entered the echoing hollowness of Liverpool Cathedral. It was overwhelming. Soaring pillars of tawny pink sandstone, huge stained-glass windows, their myriad colours reflected on the smooth grey stone floor, a welter of beauty for a sensitive seventeen-year-old, a fitting place for God to dwell. Surely, I thought, God Himself is present here.

Mother and Fiona had entered by another door, and I stood alone for a moment almost afraid to advance into such a place. Then a lady from the church fussed forward, led me into a corner, pinned a veil over my newly washed hair and straightened my dress. 'You haven't got any gloves!' she exclaimed, throwing up her hands. I looked down at my work-reddened hands and then at the hands of the other boys and girls, standing soberly near me. Everyone had on white gloves, except me. I blushed to the roots of my hair. All the sense of oneness with the beauty around me vanished. Would God ever forgive the lack of white gloves?

It was my fault. I had never thought of gloves. I blamed myself, never thinking that Mother, experienced in all things appertaining to etiquette, might have reminded me.

'I suppose you'll have to go without,' said the lady testily. 'Pull your sleeves down as far as you can.'

Hanging my head, I stood alone in a corner, waiting to be marshalled into a procession according to height, and tried to turn my thoughts again to the spiritual aspect of the ceremony, but I could not recapture it. All the pleasure and hope of my beautiful dress was lost, all the tender belief that I was approaching God like a bride ready to offer what little virtue I had to His service was gone, shot down by an impatient woman and the lack of a sixpenny pair of gloves. Ironically, I could have bought them myself, one of my shorthand students having paid me the night before. I began to shiver.

Two by two we advanced towards the old bishop sitting in front of the altar. We knelt before him and he placed his hands firmly on our heads, so that we should not rise prematurely. He said in a loud sonorous voice, 'Defend, O Lord, this Thy child with Thy heavenly grace, that she may continue Thine forever; and daily increase in Thy Holy Spirit, more and more, until she comes to Thy everlasting kingdom. Amen.'

I was so innocent that I expected to feel different after the magical words had been spoken. But I did not. I was still shivering, disconcerted by the importance of outward and visible signs – like gloves – as against the inward and spiritual grace which I had hoped to acquire that day.

Mary had said firmly to Mother that I must have a photograph of myself, to celebrate the event and as a keepsake, so the sixpence which could have been spent on the missing gloves was expended at the local photographer's, who took the first picture of me since I was a little child. Until I looked into his mirror when tidying myself ready for the photograph, I had, of course, no idea what I looked like, because at home we had only a small piece of broken mirror. The photograph was better than I had hoped.

The photograph shows a slender girl with small curves in all the right places. She is dressed in a plain lace gown with the uneven hem which had been fashionable a few years earlier. She has long slender fingers, delicate ankles, and small feet encased in white satin shoes. Her face, clothed in horn-rimmed spectacles too small for her, is as plain as the back of a Liverpool tram.

Chapter thirteen

I was now eighteen, going on nineteen, a plain, silent girl still struggling to stay alive, no longer quite so devoted to the church, deeply distrustful of the motives of those whose lives touched mine, a young woman without hope.

I had been promoted to the Stenographers' Room, working side by side with Miriam, thankful to be at last delivered from the sniggering girls downstairs. My shorthand was almost perfect, thanks to good evening school teaching; my typing was still very faulty because I had taught myself. I had consequently not received a rise in salary, just an improvement in status.

Miriam had for a long time worked very hard to raise money for the volunteers among her Communist associates who went to fight against Franco in the Spanish Civil War. Now, as her fingers flew over the typewriter keys, she raged that the war was lost to the Fascists and soon Europe would be plunged into a much bigger war. She threw herself impetuously into aiding the many Spanish children who had been sent to safety in England and into consoling the wounded, disillusioned returning volunteers.

There was a number of active Communists on our staff, earnest women toiling as social workers in the depths of Liverpool's appalling slums. Despite their desire to recruit to their party, I kept well back from their political endeavours, partly from the fact that my personal life was so full of work that I could not cope with anything as abstract as political beliefs, and partly because of the scarifying stories Father had told me of Communist excesses he had seen during his military service in Russia.

Several stenographers had come and gone during my employment with the Charity, but the Head Typist was still the devout Roman Catholic who tried regularly to save Miriam from her misbegotten ideas and me from the clutches of a heretic church. She was a dear and almost everybody was fond of her, no matter how cross she got about hanging participles and bad spelling. Between her and Miriam I learned to disagree with other people's beliefs and yet have respect for them.

At one point the Charity was so short of funds that she instituted a fine of one penny for every sheet of paper that Miriam and I wasted as a result of typing errors. Miriam promptly said, 'Not bloody likely!' and since I had little money to spare to pay fines, we smuggled screwed up balls of paper containing our typing sins out of the room, by quietly stuffing them into our overall pockets or down our necks. Occasionally, we had the most remarkably lumpy figures.

My life had settled into a dull, fatiguing rut. Ever fearful of unemployment, I clung to my job. Each January or February, I went down with influenza or bronchitis and, in my emaciated state, usually took a month to recover. The Presence always sent my wages to me, no matter how many weeks I was away, a rare generosity in those days.

A few more jobs were becoming available in the beleaguered city. Shadow factories were being built, with an eye to war; and an army of bricklayers and other building workers, though thankful for a small pay packet, cursed with pain as their blistered hands and aching backs got used to working again.

I began to have a faint glimmering of hope that, despite my lack of education, I might be able to find a better job or, by continuing my evening school studies, become well enough informed to join the more privileged green-overalled social workers.

Students came to our office from the Social Science Department of the university, to do some practical work. Our workers gave them lectures, taught them how to interview and took them to see our clients in their homes. Some of the students were horrified at what they saw and were afraid of visiting alone.

In the Committee Room a large bookcase began to be filled with volumes on the theories of social science. Whenever the lecturer forgot to lock the bookcase, I borrowed books for a night or two and read them, slipping them back into the bookcase when the room was empty. Sometimes the theories and the interpretations of statistics made me laugh, and I thought of the shrewd exploiters of social assistance amongst whom I lived. Some of our neighbours knew every trick and used extremely agile brains to obtain what they needed from the many agencies in the city; it was almost like a business to them. They were all poor, but it was often not the most needy who received the most help. Now, three generations later, this swindling has become an art, and some people live very comfortably with it. They would probably do equally well if they turned their astuteness towards earning a living. Crying poverty, however, can be a good excuse for shrugging off the weight of responsibility for one's life.

The books opened up to me the world of theory, and I began to understand that there were people who spent their lives trying to find the underlying principles upon which society and nature itself were built. Pondering upon theological questions was something to which my history reading had introduced me; now I became interested in what might be going on in the university. It was further intensified by a casual conversation with one of our older students, who told me that he had been a weaver for twelve years and had, during that time, managed to study enough to matriculate. He had also saved enough to put himself through university. For a moment my ambitions soared. Then he said, 'I couldna ha' done it without me Mam and Dad. They just asked a bit for me food – and they gave me a room to work in – you need a room of your own to do aught. Me Dad was really good. He went without to buy me books and me Mam took in washing. Soon I'll be able to help them.'

The ambition flopped like a balloon with a leak. My parents took from their girls; they did not give. They might occasionally encourage verbally, but they would not help. Any money they had, any ambition they felt, was channelled to the boys. Fiona, Avril and I were always just useful wage earners.

Alan, nearly six feet tall, though very thin, joined the Auxiliary Air Force and clumped about in strong black Air Force boots. He shone them to a jetty perfection every Sunday morning. He had an Air Force uniform, with brass buttons which were also polished with the aid of endless tins of Brasso. He learned to press his uniform himself, a radical decision brought about because once when pressing his trousers I had burned a hole in them.

Every Saturday and Sunday, he went to an airfield to be trained, first in ordinary drills and physical fitness programmes, then to work, as he said, on *real* aircraft with *real* tools. The planes were Hawker Hind biplanes, which went all of one hundred and seventy miles an hour. He was thrilled, and concentrated on the work with passionate intensity. His thin wrists strengthened as he learned to use tools, and the regular exercise broadened his shoulders. He began to walk with more self-assurance. He was paid for his service and was allowed to keep the money in addition to his pocket money.

He was generous by nature, and he would often treat the younger children to the Saturday matinée at the Rialto Cinema. They ate ice cream sandwiches during the intermission and had a wonderful time shrieking encouragement to film heroes like Tom Mix as, on his white horse, he galloped after the 'baddies', who always rode black horses.

Fiona, after spending two miserable weeks in suspense, had been engaged by the magazine dealer and was very happy, working the addressograph and, when business was slack, reading all the magazines, from *True Confessions* to *Good Housekeeping*, not to speak of a number of American magazines for men, which, she told me, were utterly shocking. Her employers treated her like one of the family. She was soon earning fifteen shillings a week, the same as me. She paid half of it to Mother for her food and kept the rest for travelling expenses and pocket money. Mother still bought her clothes, which put her away ahead of me financially.

Every night she went to bed with her hair in curling rags, until she could afford a permanent wave. I wanted such a wave, too, but had not the faintest hope of being able to afford it. I had no time to put my hair in rags, so I still had long hair pulled back into a bun.

Her boy friends multiplied, so her entertainment was paid for by a series of devoted swains. Sometimes, she would beg me to tell a more ambitious one at the front door that she was out, while she slipped through the back door to meet someone else. Her social life became one of the first family jokes at which we all laughed.

It was apparent to me that Father was now earning more than he used to. He, too, began to have a modest social life, when he met his colleagues at various public houses in the city. Several times he went to concerts at the Philharmonic Hall, newly rebuilt after a disastrous fire, which Brian and Tony had enjoyed watching. He managed to buy a suit and an overcoat and occasionally shoes and shirts.

Cinemas bored him, so he did not go to them. He did not give any more money to the home, which caused constant flareups between Mother and him. His main argument was that to retain his job he had to have a minimum of clothing, which he would certainly never get if he did not buy it himself. To that end he had to save some money. Mother would come flying back at him, that he smoked and drank too much, to which he would promptly retort that she spent most of her evenings at the cinema – she went at least twice a week – and that she also smoked like a proverbial chimney. Then they would rake up every possible transgression since the day of their marriage, and accuse and counter-accuse until the family fled or was reduced to tears and impassioned pleas to them to stop.

Though Mother was now very strong physically, she was feeling the effect of the change of life, something I had never heard of until Miriam mentioned it in connection with her mother. Mother's temper was so unpredictable that if she was more unbalanced than usual we did not notice it. She complained, however, of being overly hot and she sometimes looked as if she had fever. Miriam called these attacks hot flushes and advised me to be patient with her and encourage her to rest. I made a great effort to hold my tongue when she was being particularly vicious in her remarks, and tried to help more in the house when she obviously did not feel well.

At nearly nineteen I was an adult and better able than I had been to assess soberly what was happening to any of us. Once Mother realised that I understood what was happening to her, she seemed glad to be able to speak frankly to me about it. I encouraged her to see the doctor from time to time, and though there was no real aid then for this intense physical upheaval, he was able to comfort her by assuring her that it would pass.

Rest was possible, because she did not work full time, and when all the children were at school she could go to bed in the afternoon and get up late in the morning. Whatever cleaning and washing there was to be done was usually achieved at the weekend when I was at home. She began again to read regularly, and drew real enjoyment from the great storytellers of the time – Edgar Wallace, Jeffrey Farnol, P. G. Wodehouse, Rafael Sabatini and many others. She had been a librarian before her marriage and she liked to discuss what she had read. In me she found a willing listener.

Through her guardian, who owned a string of private libraries, she had met many of the early twentieth century writers and in those days had read much more deeply than she did in her later years. It dawned on me that her knowledge of literature had in part guided me, because every time I was ill – which was at least twice a year – she would bring me her own choice of books from the public library to read in bed. It was she, I recollected, who had brought me the first books I read on Japanese and Chinese history and travel books on South America, a continent I had never thought about before then and a fascinating area for further study.

This shared love of books formed a slender bridge

between us, and I began to find it easier to talk to her, though on a shallow level, about other concerns in which I was interested, like the war we were all afraid would break out and about the refugees pouring in from Europe.

Mother feared for her sons. She dreaded them being butchered as her own generation had been, though I once heard her remark that she had 'done her duty to the nation by producing four sons.' The idea that to produce soldiers was the duty of a mother shocked me beyond measure, but to women of her age, of the officer class, it must have seemed natural.

As a result of the battle-axes being laid down between us, though never buried, at the time of the office Christmas dance I felt brave enough to say that for once I would like to attend.

'Do you think you could help me buy a second-hand dress?' I begged humbly. 'I have never been to the office parties before, and Miriam thinks I should – I might meet some of the Committee members – and that might help me with promotion later on.' Miriam was nothing if not practical, despite her ideals.

Mother pondered over this, and said, 'I'll see.'

A few days later, she came home with a long white rayon taffeta dress, which she had bought from a girl she knew in one of the stores. My share of the cost – five shillings – was paid in two instalments, as my shorthand student paid me. The material of the dress was delicately patterned in fine red and green stripes and at the back it had long ruffles running from waist to hem. The sleeves were short and puffed and the low V-neck had a diamante clasp tucked into it. Though it was not particularly fashionable, it fitted me and Fiona said it looked quite pretty.

The white stockings bought for my Confirmation had, because of their colour, survived Fiona's marauding, so they were ready to hand, and Mother gave me the pawn ticket so that I could retrieve the white satin slippers and the petticoat from Uncle's.

The pawnbroker was Jewish, portly. What hair he had was curled tightly round a bald patch. The light of the bare electric bulb above his high counter shone on his olive face and made his heavy watch chain glitter. He was an old friend.

While the apprentice went up into the loft to retrieve the cloth-wrapped bundle, I told him shyly about the dance, and then confided that I had not been to a dancing class since I was eleven and feared I might not be able to dance.

'T' boys'll soon learn yez,' he assured me with a grin. 'Eee, now, I wish I could coom meself. But me wife'll never let me off the hook, yer know. Proper hard case she is.'

I laughed. 'I think the girls are allowed to bring a boy friend – but, of course, I haven't got one.'

'Aye, give yerself time, luv. You'll soon find one.'

I smiled, feeling suddenly a little flattered by his pleasantries, though I did not think that boy friends were likely to enter my life.

*

I sat quietly on a chair at the edge of the dance floor

for the entire evening, watching the colourful dancers.

'What else can you expect?' I asked myself. The other girls had each brought a partner. Miriam did not come, having Party affairs to attend to. Except for an elderly gentleman, who, after bowing and making a polite inquiry, brought me a dish of ice cream and a glass of lemonade, I was left alone. After a few moments of laboured remarks about the inclemency of the weather, the gentleman was drawn away by a more thoughtless and equally bored Committee member. I ate my ice cream and sipped the lemonade with what I hoped was a look of jaded sophistication, and at about half-past ten I went to the ladies' cloakroom and retrieved my old brown coat and outdoor shoes. After putting on these shabby garments, I put a carefully reserved silver threepenny piece in the attendant's saucer. She looked up from her knitting and said, 'Thank you, Miss,' a slight surprise in her thick, Liverpool voice.

It was drizzling as I dawdled back up the hill from the city restaurant in which the dance had been held. I held up the long dress from the wet pavement and the satin shoes hung from the fingertips of my other hand. Occasionally, I heaved a great sigh. The whole great expense had been for nothing.

Only Mother was up when I entered the living room. She was sitting with her feet braced high against one side of the big kitchen fireplace, her dress slipped back above her knees, to ease her veins. She laid her book down on her lap, and asked, 'Well, how was it?'

'A flop,' I replied, laying the precious slippers carefully down on a chair. 'I didn't get a dance.'

'You didn't stay till the end? It's only eleven now.'

'I could not sit there – through the night – until one in the morning – it would be too humiliating. Not one of the girls even spoke to me.'

Mother bit her lips. 'I'm sorry, dear,' she said, and she sounded as if she really was. Then after a moment, as I peeled off my coat, she added some sound advice. 'You'll have to stop looking like a frozen rabbit. Men don't like plain girls – and girls who look both plain and dull never get anywhere. You must smile – look gay.'

I sighed, and tried to smile. 'I expect you're right,' I agreed.

The next day the pretty dress, the petticoat and the beloved white satin shoes were bundled up in a white cloth and returned to Uncle.

Chapter fourteen

Nineteen-thirty-eight was the year that Mr Neville Chamberlain, our Prime Minister, sold Czechoslovakia down the river, in order to gain time for us. The word 'appeasement' entered our vocabulary, appeasement of a raving lunatic called Adolf Hitler, who with his Panzer divisions was mopping up the map of Europe. It seemed that after every visit Alan made to the cinema, he would remark that the Paramount news reels had shown the takeover of another country.

At first we all felt a sense of relief when an ailing Mr Chamberlain, supported by his black umbrella, came home from Europe and announced, 'Peace in our time'. It was peace bought at the expense of Czechoslovakia; and it seemed that gradually in the city a great sense of shame welled up. 'Letting a pack of bloody gorillas loose on them,' I heard a station porter say angrily.

The sacrifice *did* gain us time, we all knew that, time to mobilise the fleet, time to extend the barracks just off Princes Road, to fill factories at Speke with the machinery of war, expand the fire brigade, plan the evacuation of the city, time to write innumerable pamphlets which fluttered through our letter box on what to do in an air raid, gas attack, food shortage, petrol rationing, evacuation of school children – it went on and on.

A pile of gas masks in neat cardboard boxes arrived on our living room table, to make the children giggle and shiver nervously as we tried them on, and were suddenly converted into anonymous, long-snouted aliens.

It was taken for granted that if we had to go to war our cities would within a few days be flattened by air raids. Liverpool was our paramount western port, a legitimate target. I found that I was not much afraid at the prospect of death, only of being half dead beneath a mountain of rubble. I wondered if in such a situation I could commit suicide by swallowing my tongue as it was said the poor suffering Ethiopians did. Death – to be dead – did not seem to be much worse than being alive.

Mother fervently thanked God that only Alan was old enough to be called up. Alan was wildly excited, and spent every moment he could at the airfield. Father, who had fought the war to end all wars, looked particularly pinched and sad as he read the headlines in the *Echo*. He went out and bought himself a small atlas from the local tobacconist, and with more perception of the future than our army generals, spent evenings plotting the advance of the Japanese in China, a fray which had been pushed to the back pages of the papers.

I had my usual dose of flu during February, and it left me with a cough which was a nuisance to the whole family. I determined to try to save up for a holiday. I discovered from a book at work that there was a Girls' Holiday Home on the seafront at Hoylake in the Wirral, across the river. They charged about a pound for a week's stay, not a very large sum, though it would take me a long time to save it, and the shilling or so train fare.

I instituted an iron discipline. No trams at all, no twopenny cinema shows of old films at the Central Hall, only a penny bun for lunch instead of a three-penny soup, and, most difficult of all, making my easily laddered rayon stockings last longer – the main difficulty was keeping them out of the clutches of Fiona and Mother. They cost ninepence a pair and were my biggest single expense. I relooped ladders with the aid of a darning needle, an eye-straining, time-consuming job. I darned and redarned the heels, which badly fitting secondhand shoes tended to wear through very quickly. The money saved was carried in a little cloth bag on a string round my neck, and no matter how much Mother whined I never ad-mitted its existence.

After a bitter battle, Mother managed to squeeze out of me a further two shillings and sixpence from my small wages. This left me with exactly one shilling to cover all my needs, and in a desperate position. Any money for my own existence had to be earned by teaching shorthand to pupils in their homes.

Six or seven shillings would feed a woman quite well. What I ate at home would cost about three shillings, so Mother was doing quite well out of me. My one joy during this period was going to the theatre with my friend, Sylvia, the money for which was provided to all the staff by a kindly Greek inter-ested in the work of the Charity who employed me. I used to live for those evenings spent tucked up on the topmost bench of the Liverpool Repertory Theatre, one of the finest repertory theatres in the country.

The village in which the Girls' Holiday Home was situated was the village in which Grandma lived. I had spent many months of childhood with her. I used to cuddle up by her side while she taught me to read from the Bible; and, from dog-eared sheets of music, how to read the notes.

Grandma was short, plump, and always dressed in black silk or satin, skirts almost touching the floor, a boned, white lace modesty vest filling the neckline in a long vee-shape from her tiny pink ear tips to her waist. She had a hearty, merry laugh and could be very witty. As she shook her head the front curls of her snowy wig bounced gently on her forehead. When she went out to shop in the village a huge hat was skewered with long hat pins on to the top of the wig. The hat was always heavily trimmed with black, grey or white satin, sometimes held by a large diamante brooch or by a bunch of dark red cherries – very dashing – or black feathers. Because going to Liverpool to buy a new hat was an exhausting operation, my two aunts who lived with her would periodically retrim her hats for her. I accepted as natural that her clothes were always black, as were those of her very dignified circle of lady friends. Widows wore black, and a few of the older ones wore tiny black bonnets like Queen Victoria's, with a black veil which could shroud the face or be flung back, according to the official depths of one's mourning. Victoria had set the fashion for widows, a fashion nearly as repressive as that for widows in India. Grandma had been a widow for forty years. In its almost unbearable boredom, it must have seemed to such a lively woman like a life prison sentence.

Dare I go to see Grandma while I was in Hoylake, I wondered. I had dreamed for years of doing so, had wanted to run away to her when first I faced the appalling poverty of Liverpool. Father had not attempted to get into touch with her, as far as I knew, since their final quarrel when he went bankrupt, and of latter years I had refrained from visiting her because of his bitter remarks that I would not be welcome. But Father was her baby, who had arrived long after his nearest sister, and they must sometimes have wanted very much to see each other. He had also managed to quarrel furiously with his two sisters who lived with her. They did not approve of the gay life he had led nor did they approve of Mother, who, they felt, was not quite a lady, having worked for her living.

During our early years in Liverpool, a small parcel postmarked Hoylake, would arrive from time to time. It always contained a pair of very soft, finely knitted children's combinations; there was never any note. Avril or Edward would rejoice for weeks in the warm comfort of the garments. Mother always wrote a polite thank-you note to Grandma -- nothing more. I wondered sometimes what Grandma thought about during the long afternoons when she must have sat, as was her custom, in her sunny lace-curtained sitting room, cat on knee, and knitted. Did she grieve? Or was she sustained by righteous indignation? Had she any inkling at all about what was happening to us, that we looked like children who had suffered in an Indian famine?

After a noisy row with Mother about my duplicity in saving for a holiday and about my grim determination to go on it, regardless of the fact that Edward needed new shoes, it was with mixed feelings that I carried a shopping bag containing a change of clothes down the long slope of King's Gap to the sea. It was said that King William's troops set sail for Ireland from here, to fight the Battle of the Boyne, a battle celebrated annually by Liverpool Protestants with a great procession, in defiance of Roman Catholic wrath.

The wind from Liverpool Bay blew my hat off as I turned to walk along the Promenade. Along here, in a bright red brick house which was a nursing home, I had been born in a bed relinquished to my labouring mother by a wounded soldier, who lay on the floor in the passage while I yelled my first unhappy breath. Because the nursing home staff were swamped by wounded men, this man tended my mother and washed my nappies for her, while Father fought in Russia and did not know for a long time that I was born.

I ran my hand along the iron rail of the Promenade. Here, as a six-year-old, I had squeaked delightedly when a young fisherman picked me up and ran agilely along the top of the iron railings while the incoming tide lashed at the wall below us. From here, I had once or twice sailed out in his fishing boat with his brothers. The boat was a bouncing cockle of a craft which stank of fish. No wonder I am never seasick; my introduction to the sea was so happy. Grandma must have wondered once or twice why my discarded clothes smelled so badly. I never told her because officially I was spending the day with a lonely small boy who lived on the sea front. I did not like him, so when sent trustingly down the road to his house, I just went on to the beach and messed about amongst the fishing fleet, if it was in.

As far as I could see, there was no fishing fleet any more, not a sign of a sail or a net; only small pleasure craft heeled half over in the sand, waiting for the tide to come ripping in past the Hoyle Bank and round Hilbre Island and set them dancing.

The Holiday Home was spartan, but I rejoiced in clean sheets and shining floors. I was allotted a small windowless cubicle in which to sleep. It was stuffy with much use, and the whole building smelled of a mixture of floor polish, cabbage and cats.

I left the door of the cubicle open and sat down on the narrow bed and read innumerable notices on the wall telling me not to sit on the bed, to turn off the light, to be in at ten p.m., not to smoke, to come to meals promptly, etc. I wondered what to do. Girls cursing under their breath stumbled past to other cubicles, pushing heavy suitcases ahead of them.

The near darkness of the cubicle was becoming depressing, when suddenly the suitcases of two girls jammed in the narrow passageway. They swore ripely and richly in strongly accented German. Then they stood and laughed at each other. I jumped up eagerly to lend a hand, and between the three of us we managed to move the cases, though we left a long scratch on the varnished wall of the passage.

The girls were the daughters of Swiss hoteliers. They had been working in England for nearly a year as servants, in order to perfect their English. Their employers had sent them to the Holiday Home while they themselves took a vacation. They, too, had very little money. We were reciprocally pleased with each other. I could understand their German and they could follow my accentless English. It was a joy to me to show them the Wirral.

At low tide, carrying our shoes and some sandwiches, we paddled out to Hilbre Island, stopping to watch the shrimps tickling our toes, and the local people bent double as they dug for cockles and mussels. We watched the sea roar in again round the tiny island, while we hunted for seashells along its shore. In the evening, when the water had silently retreated, we strolled slowly back across the wet sand, while the hills of North Wales went purple and the lights of West Kirby began to wink out ahead. As we walked, I pointed out to them the stumps of a great primeval forest sticking out of the sand, and we imagined tiny brown men in coracles drifting round the mouths of the Dee and the Mersey.

Puffing in the boisterous wind, we walked the length of the great seawall which held back the tide from the villages of Moreton and Leasowe. Behind the wall rich market gardens showed neat squares of different shades of green. Dutch dike specialists came from time to time to inspect this great sea wall and it was much admired. Father used to say that the best cure for a cold was to walk its length and let the wild clean air from the Bay blow the germs out, which probably was not quite what the builders had in mind.

We scrambled down into an abandoned quarry, in the hope of finding some of the nests of the innumerable birds who made it their home. We did not find a nest and we had a panicky few minutes before we managed to haul ourselves out, dusty, breathless and laughing. There were no birds except sparrows in our street in Liverpool, and the riotous singing in that quarry was like a Polish choir going full belt.

Inland, we discovered small villages in winding lanes, and we would walk along them singing softly together, enjoying the great swishing trees and eating penny ice creams bought from minute village shops.

I was happy with my gay companions. Good though very plain food helped my famished body, and the cough lessened. But all the time I thought of Grandma.

One day we passed along the road in which she lived, three giggly, gawky girls, two in light sleeveless summer dresses, one in a winter skirt and crumpled blouse, and I glanced quickly, almost frightenedly, at the house which meant so much to me.

It looked exactly the same as I remembered it. Lace curtains draped round the windows, wrought-iron gate, straight red-tiled path to the front door, carefully swept and washed, and a patch of neatly cut lawn with a few recalcitrant daisies scattered on it like stars.

I do not know why it is that some front doors look more closed than other shut doors, but to me Grandma's door looked that day particularly blank and forbidding. I did not sleep much during the night as I wondered whether if I knocked and it were opened, there would be any welcome inside.

Towards the end of the week, the two Swiss girls became acquainted with two young men who had been caulking a rowing boat on the shore. I had walked up to the village to buy a small gift for Mother, a peace offering.

On the Friday, the girls received an invitation from the boat caulkers to go out for a row, so I had my last afternoon in Hoylake to myself. At first I sat in the gloom – on my bed – and read the notice which said that one should not use the bedroom in the daytime. I felt very lonely in the deserted Home, and chewed my thumb unhappily.

Then, as if propelled by instinct alone, I got up and quickly washed my hands and face in the communal bathroom, changed my blouse, galloped down the stairs and ran along the Promenade, not pausing for breath until I was faced with the slope of King's Gap. My battered handbag was clutched in one hand, while with the other I tried to stop the hairpins falling out of my hair in the playful breeze.

Breathless, I opened the gate and ran up the familiar path, as if afraid that if I were observed from the windows someone would stop my entering.

I knocked.

There was no response. Perhaps everyone was out.

Shyly, I knocked again, and there was the sound of the well-remembered step of one of my aunts.

She opened the door, looked at me blankly, and then smiled. 'Why, Helen!' she exclaimed.

Still panting, I asked, 'Is Grandma at home?'

My aunt hesitated, and then said, 'Yes, she is. Do come in.'

I entered and paused in the doorway, while the feeling of the house rushed over me. The grandfather clock was still ticking its friendly tick, the house still smelled sweetly of flowers, polish and women's perfumes. No odour of tobacco or cooking. The antique china pieces still decorated a small shelf above the sitting room door, through which my aunt had vanished, her pink-striped Macclesfield silk dress flicking behind her, as she shut the door after her.

As breath returned to me, panic also invaded. What was I going to talk about?

My aunt was back in the hall, and saying, 'Go in, Helen.' She gestured with one thin, delicate hand. She closed the door behind me as I went in, and I could hear her going upstairs. I felt the same fear that I always did when the Presence sent for me to scold me for typing errors.

The room was shadowed in comparison with the bright sunshine outside, and for a second I could hardly see the figure seated near the fireplace in one of the chintz-covered easy chairs.

I caught my breath sharply, as if someone had stabbed me with a pin.

A tiny, shrunken person, swathed in black seemed engulfed in the chair. Beneath a white wig which appeared too large, two dim blue eyes smiled at me in a face hung with paperwhite folds of skin. The familiar brooch on the lace under her chin looked big and clumsy. Hands which seemed only bone and blue veins rested on a shallow china bowl of green peas, and on a small table by the chair was a basket full of pea shells and a brown paper bag, which presumably held more of the vegetable.

I stood awkwardly in front of her. 'Granny,' I said, while inside my heart cried. I had forgotten what great age did to the human frame. To me she was eternal. I was suddenly and brokenly aware of all the years that I had missed being with her. She was in her nineties, and though I did not care very much about death for myself, I wanted her to live for ever.

'How very nice,' she said, in a weak but clear voice. 'Come here, dear.'

I went to her and carefully kissed the papery cheek. She smelled sweetly of Yardley's lavender, as usual, and her lace modesty vest was fresh and white. 'Sit down, dear, and tell me about yourself. Bring that chair close to me.'

So I brought a straight chair and sat knee to knee with her. While we shelled peas together, I told her about the Holiday Home and about my job and how I hoped one day to be a social worker. Somehow, I could not bring myself to tell her about the frightful privation we had endured, nor about the steady hunger and cold, the lack of blankets, woollens and coal from which we still suffered. She had obviously been ill and I was not too certain that she comprehended all that I was saying to her.

When the peas had all been shelled, she leaned her head against the back of the chair and closed her eyes. I stopped talking, and she reached out her hand. I held the fragile fingers, while she rested, and thought about a small girl whose hand she had held through many a walk to the village. Now, it was I who was holding her hand.

After a while, my aunt came briskly into the room, and said, 'It's time for your walk, Mother.' She picked up the bowl of peas, the brown paper bag and the basket of shells. 'Perhaps Helen would like to go with you.'

'Certainly,' I agreed.

Grandma opened her eyes and looked at me. There was a slight twinkle in them. 'Yes. We'll go together. It will give Aunt Emily a rest.'

A long black coat was brought in by Aunt Emily and the old lady was eased into it. Carpet slippers were exchanged for tiny button shoes, which Aunt Emily did up. A hat as monumental as I ever remembered, trimmed with a touch of white – Grandma's only acknowledgment of summer – was carefully pinned on by Grandma herself. Then she sat down on a straight chair for a moment to recover from the exertion.

'How long for, Auntie?' I asked.

'About half an hour. Keep off the Promenade. The wind is too much for her.'

I nodded, and she opened the door for us. Grandma carefully crept across the rugs, and I eased her down the single step. She shuffled forward along the red-tiled path.

It seemed a terribly long way to the gate, and miles to the end of the road. However, Grandma silently concentrated on walking, and we turned into King's Gap, away from the sea. After about five minutes on the gentle slope, Grandma gasped, 'I think I have to sit down, dear.'

'Oh, goodness!' I looked wildly round for a bench or a low wall. The nearest place was a wooden seat about a hundred yards away. I pointed it out.

Grandma was panting, her mouth a little open. 'It seems a long way.'

'It is closer than returning home, Granny. I could carry you.'

She smiled up at me with the bright flash that I had known as a child, as if her mind had reverted to its old clarity. 'No, no. Don't be afraid, my dear. We will do it a step at a time.'

It was the longest hundred yards I have ever walked, but we finally got there and sank thankfully on to the weathered seat. I put my arm around Grandma's shoulder and she leaned against me and closed her eyes. It was like holding a small sheaf of wheat, the same sense of easy crushability.

I looked down at the top of the satin-trimmed hat, now pushed askew because she had laid her head on my shoulder. My old enemy, despair, washed over me. Memories shot through my mind, a belief in her inherent goodness, gratitude for the skills she had passed to me. She had taught me more subtle things than reading and sewing, to put on a cheerful face so that one does not depress others, to face with fortitude what cannot be changed, daily courtesies, which always surfaced when I was with people of my own class. My aunts, too, had been very patient with a silent, obstinate little girl.

Now I knew in my heart that Grandma had come

close to the end of her allotted span, and I did not know how to face the idea. I wanted to wrap her up in cotton wool, like something infinitely precious that must be preserved at all costs.

But nothing I could do would stop the remorseless march of the years – and it was obvious that the aunts were caring for her very well.

The return was accomplished by slow shuffles and pauses, a trifle more easily since the mild slope was downwards. Grandma did not say much, except for an occasional deprecating chuckle at her own inadequacies as she stopped to pant.

The front door opened as we approached up the path, and I pushed Grandma ahead of me up the step. She stopped for a second when safely landed, and then toddled into the hall. My aunt said, 'Thank you very much indeed for taking her out. She has to rest now.' She began to close the door, and added, with a bright smile, 'It must be your tea time by now.' Then she quietly shut the door.

I looked dumbly at the blank piece of wood in front of my nose, hardly able to believe that it was truly shut. A slow burning flush flooded my face and I turned angrily away and marched down the hill to the sea. The wind rushed up to meet me and helped to cool the fury within. I dropped over the railings of the Promenade on to the deserted powdery sands, and turned towards my favourite place, the Red Rocks.

Until the water began to lap close, I did not think of the tide cutting me off. I hastily took off shoes and stockings and paddled quickly the last few yards.

Such was the respect for property instilled into me that it never occurred to me to climb the sloping walls which protected the private gardens running down to the beach, and walk through to the road, and so save myself from the icy water.

I sat down on the rocks at a safe elevation and wrung out the hem of my heavy skirt. Then, cross-legged, chin in hand, I watched for a long time the tide race in and the sailing boats set out from Hoylake and West Kirby. I forgot about tea at the Holiday Home and was aware only of the pain inside me.

The sun sank slowly down in the centre of the sea, leaving an emerald green and bright pink sky. Grandma had a little oil painting which she said Turner had painted of that sunset. The painting was dark from years of being too close to the smoke of the fireplace, but as a child I had loved to run my fingers round its elaborately carved gilt frame.

With twilight, it became cold, so, shivering, I put on my shoes and stockings and clambered over the rocks to the road, and with head bent with grief and no little sense of humiliation I plodded along the almost deserted road back to the Home.

Chapter fifteen

At home, Mother had recovered from her vexation at my daring to go for a holiday. She was further mollified by the gift which I had brought her, a pretty box covered with sea shells. Both she and Father were intensely interested when I told them that I had been to see Grandma.

'Did she ask about us?' inquired Mother.

I looked at them both sadly, and had to admit that she had not asked a single question about the family, not even about Father.

'She's very weak,' I defended. 'I'm not sure that she is quite aware of what is going on around her. And, of course, I got cut off rather abruptly from her, when the door was shut on me. I had imagined that we would talk more over a cup of tea – or something.'

Father's voice was acidulous. 'I'm surprised they let you in.'

In June of 1939, a strange man presented himself at our door. He was small, dressed in a belted raincoat and a trilby hat. Father had answered the door and thought he was a salesman. He was just about to say, 'Not today, thank you,' when the man said, 'You must be Mr Forrester?'

Father agreed that he was.

'I am sorry to tell you that your mother has died,'

the stranger baldly announced. He then went on to say when the funeral would be held.

I had been standing on the staircase watching the scene, and the cold words bit into me. I wondered how much more they must have hurt Father. He looked very white, as he ushered the visitor into our living room. Our tenants in the front room had recently found a house and left us, so our home smelled a lot better – but the sitting room was still bare of furniture. I followed them into the living room.

Mother was introduced as the visitor edged his way into the crowded room, and when they were all seated Father asked how Grandma had died. My eyes misted, as I leaned against the door jamb. I remembered the little wraith with whom I had walked. It would not have taken much to blow her out of this life.

'She died in her sleep – from a stroke,' the visitor said. He went on to explain that she had had a stroke a year earlier and then, more recently, a series of smaller ones.

Father and Mother sat quiet for a minute. Then Father realised he had not inquired who the man was, and now he did this. The man gave his name and said he was a friend of the family. He had business in Liverpool, so had been asked to convey the news of the death to us.

Father closed his eyes. Despite the gravity of Mother's expression, there was a bright gleam in her eyes, which I did not understand.

Father said he would attend the funeral and looked inquiringly at Mother. Mother nodded negatively. 'Mrs Forrester will not attend.' He looked unhappily at me. 'If my eldest daughter wishes, she will accompany me.' I lowered my eyelids and made no response. I had not thought about the funeral.

Politenesses were exchanged and the man was ushered out. 'Unfeeling bastard,' exclaimed Father, as he came back in. He sat down slowly on his battered easy chair and put a shaky hand over his eyes.

'I'm sorry, Daddy,' I said gently. 'After all, he was a stranger – he didn't *have* to come.'

After some dithering, I decided not to go to the funeral, though as a child I had been very fond of my aunts. I was afraid they would think ill of me, because I had no mourning clothes and no money to buy any. I said to Mother, 'I would have to ask for a half day off – and every office boy who wants to go to a football match says he needs time off to go to his grandmother's funeral – and I've had so much sick leave that they might feel I was imposing on them by asking for more.'

Mother sighed, and agreed. 'Remember your grandmother as she was, dear, when you were little.'

She had understood, and she had called me 'dear'. I was grateful to her.

The day of Grandma's funeral was overcast and rainy in Liverpool. Mother stitched a black band of ribbon, culled from an old felt hat, round the left arm of Father's overcoat, a sign of mourning for those who could not afford black clothes. He shaved slowly and carefully that morning and gave his shoes a tremendous polish in a kind of dumb honour to his mother. I checked that his socks did not have holes in their heels, and wept all the way to work.

When he arrived home in the evening, he was emotionally exhausted. For once, Mother fussed round him. She made him tea, and put more coal on the fire to dry the legs of his trousers, which were soaked, as were his muddy shoes and socks which were put inside the fender to steam on the hearth. He had walked all the way to and from James Street station, because he did not have enough money for a tram, after paying the train fare to Hoylake.

'Did they give you anything to eat?' I asked, as he sipped the scalding brew from his cup.

He nodded negatively.

While Mother sat with him, I went into the kitchen, made toast, and in some bacon fat fried the solitary egg sitting on the shelf. Fortunately, all the children had gone out to friends' houses to play, so the house was quiet.

Father was not accustomed to so much attention, and after he was warmed and fed and had returned to sit in his easy chair, he cheered up a little.

'They all stood on one side of the grave – and I stood on the other. I felt like a pariah. Nobody spoke to me, except the solicitor, who said I had better come back to the house with them for the reading of the will.'

Again I saw the sudden gleam in Mother's eye – and this time I understood it. Grandma had quite an estate to leave. The unlit cigarette between her lips quivered.

Father sighed heavily. 'You will remember that years ago, my brothers and I signed an agreement that the contents of Mother's home should not be broken up but would be left to my sisters, so that they were assured of a home.' He paused and took off his spectacles to rub his eyes. Then he laughed, a small deprecating laugh. 'That was before your uncles died – and in the days when we had a home worth speaking of.'

Mother nodded. She tore a piece of newspaper from the *Echo* on her lap and started absently to fashion it into a spill.

'Well, of course, that still holds,' continued Father. 'Then in her will she left all her own property – that's the dowry she brought with her when she married father, to the aunts, so as to give them a better income to live on, I suppose – I don't think they have a great deal themselves.'

Mother leaned towards the fire to light the spill and then with the flame she lit her cigarette, puffed and blew the smoke towards the blackened ceiling.

'What about your reversionary interest?' she asked.

'What on earth is a reversionary interest?' I interjected.

Father turned to me. 'Well, dear, you know your grandfather died when I was a little boy. He left all his property to your grandmother for her lifetime. This meant that she enjoyed the interest – rents – whatever else he had – but she could not touch the capital. The capital was to be divided between his children or their heirs, after your grandmother died.'

I knew my grandfather had been far from poor, and I gasped. 'Does that mean we actually get some money?'

'Well, I had hoped so, though I think that the estate has not prospered because of poor management by his executors. Anyway, the thing is that when you were young, I borrowed from one of your aunts against my interest. Not against all of it by any means.'

He stopped and stared into the fire. Then he took out a cigarette, leaned over and lit it from Mother's.

'Well, what happened?'

'I signed a legal agreement in which I promised to pay interest on the loan – I had expected to pay the loan back quite quickly. I could not repay – and I forgot about the interest until today. She claimed the interest for ten years – and that wiped out my share.'

'Good God!' exclaimed Mother, cigarette half way to her mouth. 'Did she really?'

'Yes.' Father sighed again. 'She was legally entitled to it. Only it never struck me that a sister would actually charge interest.'

I made a face. Father was so unbelievably innocent at times that I wondered how he had survived at all so far.

'Well,' I said slowly, 'I suppose if she had had the money invested all these years, she would have got interest on it – and if she had not spent it, her capital would have increased substantially.'

'True,' said Father sadly. 'She was entitled to it.'

Mother clicked her tongue in exasperation, and unthinkingly stabbed her half-finished cigarette out on the bars of the fireplace. She flung the stub angrily into the unusually cheerful blaze.

And I sat quietly thinking of my usual obsession – cold. I thought of a frigid bed, where I lay with aching limbs beside a restless Avril, whose feet seemed always to be icy, and a patient Fiona who folded her arms tight across her chest and never complained. I dreamed of white sheets and a pile of fluffy blankets piled on top of us – and, yes, a hot water bottle each. And of the boys, inadequately clad, despite their school uniforms paid for by the city, often with wet feet and no gloves. Alan at least had his Air Force boots and a really thick Air Force uniform, so that he was warm during the weekends, but he must have been cold in bed, too. Our house was jerry built and the heat of our single fire was soon dissipated.

I thought wistfully that a small capital sum, if my parents used it sensibly, would save us so much misery – though I had to admit that our present circumstances were a little better than they had been.

'Never mind, Daddy,' I tried to reassure him. 'One of these days, we will have all the basics of life again and be quite comfortable.'

He smiled at me, looking suddenly very like his mother.

Mother looked as if she were about to cry.

A few days later, a small parcel came by mail for me. It contained a watch, and it had come from Hoylake. I presumed it was Grandma's and was delighted that she had remembered me. It was a neat gold one, with a black moire ribbon wrist band, and I put it on with tender pleasure. I never left it off my wrist, so it was never pawned.

Early in the war, when I had enough money to afford it, I took the watch to a reputable jeweller to be cleaned and adjusted. He asked my name, opened the watch and took it into a back room. A moment later, he returned very fast, his face most forbidding. 'We sold this watch to . . . ' and he named my cousin. 'Please explain how you come to have it.' He waited, lips pursed, eyes accusing.

My mouth fell open with shock at the abrasive tone. I licked my lips and swallowed, not knowing what to say. I knew I still looked like a skivvy, a kind of person who would never normally have been in his shop.

'It was left to me by my grandmother,' I faltered. 'The lady you mention is my cousin who lived with her.'

'When?'

I gave the date of my grandmother's death. I was very frightened. I feared he might call the police and accuse me of theft.

'What is your cousin's address?'

I gave my grandmother's address, where I presumed she still lived, and said, trembling, 'She probably bought it as a gift for Grandma.'

The address obviously tallied with the one he had, so he said slowly, 'I see.'

He pulled out a receipt, made it out in my name and, without apology or explanation, handed it to me. 'Ready in a week,' he said.

Badly shaken, I went out of the shop and stood on the pavement and watched unseeingly the rush of lunch hour pedestrians. Because I was obviously so poor, I had been treated as a possible thief. I was outraged.

I never forgot the arrogant jeweller, and I felt a most unchristian satisfaction when his shop was blown up later in the war.

Chapter sixteen

I was nineteen going on twenty and I had never been kissed by a man, other than an occasional peck from Father. I had never gone to an adult party and only once been to a dance. I had never since I was eleven played any games, did not know the meaning of the word *fun*. It seemed as if there was nothing but work in the world. The only real pleasure was my regular visits to the Repertory Theatre with Sylvia and an occasional walk with her.

The dogs of war who were to eat my generation were howling through the streets of Europe. The basement waiting room of the Charity for which I worked was packed with woebegone, nerve-racked Jewish and Trade Union refugees from every country in Europe. Upstairs, in the Interviewing Department, lay a Dictionary of the Languages of Europe and this was handed to non-English-speaking clients, so that they could at least establish for us which country they came from and which language they spoke. We could then obtain an appropriate interpreter. My French and German, though far from perfect, became suddenly useful.

In the parks, trenches were dug as air raid shelters. I remembered stories my father's friends had told, when I was little, of flooded trenches rotten with corpses and preying rats, and I felt sick.

For my twentieth birthday on 6th June, 1939, Friedrich, my ever faithful German pen-friend, now a young officer in the Luftwaffe, sent me a small ivory edelweiss on a gold chain; in his part of Germany the edelweiss was, in the olden days, given by a boy to his prospective bride. It was a lovely gift, the first piece of jewellery that I had ever owned, except for Grandma's watch, and I sighed regretfully over it – an English woman would certainly not be approved of as a wife of a Luftwaffe officer – and I wished that he had followed his original intention of becoming a schoolmaster. With the gift came a charmingly sentimental letter. In answer to a rather depressing letter from me, he assured me that his beloved Fuehrer would never plunge Europe into war. All Herr Hitler wished was to see all German-speaking people united under one flag. One day German travel restrictions would be lifted and we would meet each other and how wonderful that would be.

It could, of course, be that Friedrich was right and all our newspapers were wrong. As an Air Force officer, he might know more than I did of what was happening. Sometimes the *Express* gave the same view as Friedrich, and it was a big newspaper – it should know.

With the edelweiss in my hand, I dreamed wistfully. He had no inkling of the many other problems which I faced. The previous Christmas I had wanted to send him a present, a real challenge for me. I solved it by buying a torn sheet from the second hand shop, for a few pennies. The sides of the sheet were still good, and from that material I had cut six

139

handkerchiefs, and hem-stitched them. The drawn-thread work was trying to the eyes, but the result was attractive. Then I embroidered Father's initials on three of them and Friedrich's on the other three. I had ringed Friedrich's monogram with a ring of tiny roses, all done with white cotton. Both recipients had been delighted.

'What on earth would Friedrich think,' I wondered, with a wry grin, 'if he knew where his gift had come from? What would he think if he saw my home?'

Our sitting room had once more been furnished on the hire purchase system, and we had finally managed to pay off the debts for which we were still responsible on the earlier sets of furniture which had been repossessed by the furniture stores. Father had also bought, on the same plan, a radio which was a great joy to all of us.

The radio ran on batteries and we had periodical crises when new batteries were required. The wet battery had to be recharged about once a week; and I soon learned, after carrying it down to the shop to have this done, to walk down the street with bare legs. The acid from the battery tended to slop down one's legs and burn them. Legs heal eventually – stockings do not. I still carry faint marks on my legs from those acid burns.

Despite the fact that five wages were now coming into the house, none of us earned very much. My parents still had little idea of how to manage a small income, with the result that we were still very poorly fed, often cold, and lacked proper changes of clothing. Shoes still got lined with cardboard to fill the holes in the soles, and I still sat at work with my feet firmly on the floor so that the other girls would not notice the holes.

Mr Ellis, with his formidable tongue, had been replaced by a gentle elderly lady, who was invariably polite and kind to me. Without saying anything, she seemed to understand a little of what was happening to me and the consistent effort I was making to educate myself. She sometimes asked me what plays I had seen – she also received theatre money, as it was called by the staff – and what books I had read recently.

Perhaps it was because of her recommendation that one morning the Presence sent for me.

'Oh, my goodness,' I groaned to Miriam. 'What have I done now?'

The Presence smiled, actually smiled, when after knocking timidly I entered her office.

'Sit down, Miss Forrester,' she ordered briskly.

Nervously I perched on the edge of her visitor's chair. If I had to sit down to hear it, she must have something quite devastating to say.

'Miss Forrester, we are expanding our Bootle office. The District Head at present runs it with the aid of voluntary workers. She does, however, need someone on whom she can rely to assist her. We have decided to appoint an Assistant District Head, and I would like to send you out there.'

I gaped. Presumably I would be a kind of Girl Friday – but the designation of the post put me close to the rank of the long envied green-overalled social workers. The post could lead to further promotion. Perhaps a living wage.

'The salary would be seventeen shillings and six-pence a week,' Miss Danson added, and swivelled herself round to look at me for the first time.

A rise in pay of half-a-crown would just cover the additional long tram journeys out to the north end of the city. It would not stretch to anything more. But it was a break at last.

I smiled. 'I would like that very much,' I assured the Presence enthusiastically, putting to the back of my mind how much the tram journeys would add to my already incredibly long working day.

Full of excitement I broke the news to Mother. She refused to believe that the rise in pay had been so little. 'It amounts to nothing, really,' she fretted. 'They must have given you at least five shillings?'

'They didn't, Mummy, I assure you. But I will get training in actual casework – and that is worth something.'

So, for half-a-crown more than I would have received had I been unemployed, I took on considerable responsibility and continued to live largely on hope.

Bootle had more unemployment, more over-crowding, more pollution, more ignorance, more huge Roman Catholic families floundering in poverty than I had ever seen before. It was even worse than the badly hit south side of the city. No wonder the patient, delicate-looking District Head needed help. With only the Society's small funds available to us, it was like being asked to shovel out a rubbish dump with a teaspoon.

I plunged in to help, but found the greatest diffi-culty was within myself. I had been so crushed by the staff of the Head Office that I tended never to do anything which I had not been asked to do. I had little natural initiative; only a kind of slave-like mentality. And this had, with much trial and error, to be slowly overcome. If I was to join the green overalls, all of whom had degrees, I realised sadly that I had a long way to go.

One night, as I sat huddled on the tram from Bootle, I pondered over my inabilities, not at that time very clear about what ailed me, knowing only that change I must from the frail, drained woman for whom nobody cared very much, into a more dynamic person. Otherwise, I feared, I did not have much to look forward to in the future.

Left alone with Father one Saturday afternoon, I asked him tentatively if he could think of any other kind of work to which I might aspire. Without a second's thought, he came up with a very good suggestion. 'You might be able to pass the entry exams for the Civil Service by now – they give you quite a wide choice of subjects, you know.'

Half believing, I made inquiries and found he was correct. Father became interested, and I found a schoolmaster willing to coach me in Geography, the weakest subject amongst the rag bag of subjects which I could offer. For five shillings a lesson, half of it contributed by Father, he came to the house in the evenings, and began to teach me about winds, tides and currents and how they affected the layout of the world. And I was hooked. Nobody in my childhood had taught me anything beyond the names of rivers, cities, countries, seas and where they were. Night school was finished for the season, and, fascinated, I studied earnestly from the books he lent me. He came four times. Then I received a brief note from his wife that he had been called up. Reluctantly I returned the books.

A few weeks later, the Civil Service cancelled its examinations for the duration of the war. Nobody seemed to know at that time how they would recruit any staff they would require.

Frustrated, I threw myself once more into an effort to improve my social work.

Chapter seventeen

As war began to breathe down the back of our necks, our socially isolated family received unexpected visitors.

A fussy, elderly man who lived in the next street arrvied to show us how to put on our gas masks. He was apologetic to the ladies because their hair styles were likely to be disturbed by the straps, since it was essential that the masks fit tightly. He recommended our keeping our hair short. He also warned us that mascara was liable to melt and run down our faces while we had our masks on.

Fiona was the only member of the family who used mascara, and she continued placidly to brush it on in front of the piece of mirror wedged into the kitchen window frame. It made her already huge eyelashes even more seductive. She brushed her hair up into the newly fashionable high sweeps round her face, and at the back bouncing curls fell to her shoulders.

My bun got so tangled up with the straps of the mask that it was as well that there never was a gas attack.

The air raid warden knocked peremptorily on our door. He lived a few doors away from us and had been unemployed for years. He had a reputation for being utterly lazy, but he took his present duties very seriously, and demanded to see our blackout curtains.

We had none. We had no curtains at all upstairs, except for a short net curtain across the front bedroom window. We did have, however, the original big wooden shutters of the house in the downstairs rooms, and had always used these instead of curtains in the living room. The warden agreed that these would make excellent blackout and a good defence against flying glass. He tutted like a maiden aunt over the bare bedroom windows, and ordered us to buy black cloth and make curtains.

'Or yer can paste double layers of brown paper over t' panes. Another thing you can do, is make wooden frames covered with thick paper and fit 'em into t' windows each night, like.'

Mother said frostily that we would just have to manage without candlelight in the bedrooms. She was not going to blot out the daylight with brown paper, and she could not afford curtains or frames.

The warden stuck his blue chin in the air and replied that the windows must be covered – by law – in case the flare of a match or other casual light flashed out of them and brought German bombs down upon us.

Mother was not going to take orders from any local oaf, and retorted, 'What rubbish!'

The warden stood firm. 'I tell yez, you'll be fined if you don't cover 'em,' he warned, his dark Irish face grim as he held his temper in.

Muttering maledictions, Mother went out to buy blackout material for the front bedroom. Then, in the copper in the basement, we dyed two of our few sheets and pinned one over the back kitchen window, which lacked shutters, and one over the window of the boys' bedroom. The girls' bedroom window remained bare and, since we could not show a light, we had to fumble round in the dark when going to bed.

The warden was not satisfied. The windows should have sticky tape crisscrossed over them, to stop shattering glass from flying into the rooms. Mother said she would see to it, but she never did, and the patient warden finally acknowledged defeat. Resignedly, he recommended that we sit on the basement steps during raids, that being the safest place in the house.

A school teacher came to explain the need to evacuate Brian, Tony, Avril and Edward to the country, in the charge of their teachers. She was a faded, middle-aged woman in a worn tweed suit, and the children stood around the room and stared at her, as she spoke.

She inquired if we had any relations to whom they could be sent. 'You might prefer that to their going with the school.' Her artificial teeth clicked as she pushed them into place with her tongue.

'No,' replied Mother. Father cleared his throat.

'There are the aunts at Hoylake,' I suggested tentatively. 'Could Avril go to them?'

'I doubt if they would take her,' Father interjected, and it was finally agreed that the children would leave with the school.

Dismayed at the thought of filthy, lousy evacuees from Liverpool or Birkenhead being billetted on them, the aunts had the same idea as I did, and the next day a letter arrived suggesting that they should take in two of the children. Father roared with laughter at the thought of how suddenly important their long-neglected nephews and nieces had become. He turned the letter over and over in his hand, and remarked, 'I can't remember when one of them wrote to me last.'

Mother looked as if she had been caught between the devil and the deep blue sea, and I tried to reassure her.

'They were always very kind to me when I was a child,' I said quickly. 'None of the children will come to harm with them.'

So, as German tanks ploughed across the Polish border, Tony and Edward, with a pitifully small amount of luggage, went off with a school teacher, to meet the aunts they had never seen. I will never forget their tight, white little faces. A stony-faced Avril, determined to be brave, went with them, to live nearby with a friend of the aunts; and for the first time in her memory knew what it was to have good, new clothes bought for her, sleep in a properly equipped bed and be decently fed. Brian, like a young soldier, went with the school to Wales and lived with a postman who was also exceedingly good to him. Despite much kindness, none of the children came through that traumatic time without scars.

The government provided an allowance for the evacuees' board. But later on, they demanded that parents contribute to this cost. On the day they announced this, Mother decided that she could not bear to be parted from her darlings any longer, and they were brought home. If she had to maintain her children, they might as well be at home, air raids notwithstanding. When the raids became very heavy, under pressure from the school, they were re-evacuated, this time to strangers, and they were very unhappy. However, when the Government again demanded money, Mother brought them home. They were thankful to return, despite the danger.

In June, 1939, Alan went gaily off, for the second year, for his annual training camp with the Auxiliary Air Force. It was to be two weeks long and was to be his holiday. We knew that, like the first one he had attended, he would be out in the countryside at a Royal Air Force base being well fed and would be enjoying himself working with tools. He would also be paid, and would return home looking well and with pocket money to spend. Before he went, he bought himself a new sports jacket and trousers, so that off duty he would look smart, and we teased him before he went, about all the feminine hearts he would break during his free evenings. He was happy.

He did not return. There was no letter to say what had happened, and Mother was in a panic. Father said that a number of young men from his office had also not returned from various military training camps where they had gone as Territorials for their summer training. It was part of the national call-up.

About a month later, the postman delivered a small sack containing Alan's unworn sports jacket and trousers. Mother wept. 'He must be dead,' she mourned, and pawned them next time she was short of money.

Father reminded her that the Forces were very good at telegraphing the news of deaths. No news was good news.

Three or four months later, he arrived home on forty-eight hours' leave. He looked even thinner than when he had left us, but it seemed as if he had grown a foot. He had finished an arduous square-bashing, through which all regular recruits had to go, and was now again thankfully working on planes. He was tired and slept most of his leave, but he was still enthusiastic and went back to his base quite cheerfully.

He had obviously had a tough training period, so we refrained from reminding him that we would have been glad of a letter to say where he was. Now we had an address, both Mother and I wrote to him regularly.

Mother forbade me to write to the evacuated children or to go to see them. I was very angry about this, but gave in sulkily when she said, 'Seeing someone from home will upset them.' Despite her argument, she went out to Hoylake to see them and she would never say how she got on with her in-laws. I could not really understand her objection to my going, but she may have been jealous for a long time of my particular position as surrogate mother, and wished to reassert herself with them.

Anyway, I obeyed. I was finding it increasingly hard to face up to Mother. My new job amid appalling squalor, in addition to the long journey out to Bootle, was draining a character already crushed and exhausted.

It seemed as if the whole population of the country was on the move, as men were called up and women shut down their homes and went back to live with mother, as the children vanished into the countryside, and drafted workers got sent to distant war factories. Lonely youths far from home spent much time cultivating girls who would invite them to their homes, to compensate a little for spartan Victorian barracks or bare, comfortless workers' dormitories. Fiona's dates multiplied exceedingly, and into our emptied house began to drift a curious assortment of men of all nations and all social classes, to eat our rations and warm their wet feet at our single fire, to have their socks darned and their buttons stitched on. Mother was in her element as a hostess, and we all hoped, as the war progressed and the other boys were called up, that somewhere in the world Alan, Brian and Tony were being taken care of, too. I think this was the best contribution that Mother ever made to society, as she tried to feed and comfort the strangers at our door.

Chapter eighteen

To say that in the summer of 1939 we were scared would have been an understatement. Almost everybody in Liverpool was obsessed by a dread of the unknown. The tenseness of men's voices and their slightly hysterical laughter, the grim shut-in look of women whose sons and husbands were being called up, the problems of beleaguered city officials suddenly faced with putting into effect elaborate programmes, which had been concocted by equally harassed civil servants sitting at desks in far away London, all contributed to an almost unbearable tension as we waited.

Much preliminary work had already been done during the year of time bought for us by Mr Chamberlain during the infamous meeting in Munich in 1938. Now, there was a great urgency, and everybody's life was thrown into confusion.

Father was transferred by the City to work amongst the increasing number of refugees from Europe, who were arriving in Liverpool. He was shortly to be nearly overwhelmed by the arrival, in waves, of battered contingents of the Polish Army and Air Force. Later, he was transferred to the staff dealing with the inadequate Rest Centres provided for the bombed-out. They had originally been meagerly provisioned to discourage people from settling down to live in them rather than seeking new accommodation. The frantic needs of bewildered households, often without menfolk, could not be met. The more houses that were damaged, the more people crowded the Rest Centres and the less likelihood they had of finding alternative accommodation. Father worked like a demon.

In the meantime, we waited, fearing the future and yet unable to visualise what it would bring. Mother had been working as the representative of a greetings card firm. In August, she found herself politely dismissed, in the expectation that the paper for such a business would be severely rationed. She decided that she could, now the children were away, take a full-time post, and she was thankfully snapped up by a big bakery firm, whose bookkeeper, a Naval Reservist, had vanished into the navy. Mother could keep books because, at one point, during the First World War, just before my birth, she had taken the place of a man in a bank, and she said that she was the first lady cashier in Liverpool. The salary offered seemed enormous in comparison with what the rest of us were earning, and she was able to buy herself some new clothes and send some extra clothing to our frightened little evacuees at the aunts' house. We now had five less mouths to feed, and this made a great difference. I had cornflakes for breakfast as well as a piece of bread and margarine, and occasionally marmalade, which I had not tasted for many years. There was no shortage of food in the shops and we were not rationed until several months later.

This better salary which Mother was able to command made me even more ambitious to join the ranks of the green-overalled social workers. But the longer I worked in the Bootle office the more I realised that lack of education was going to hold me back. Anyone new coming on to staff had a degree. It was not that I could not do the work. I understood only too well most of the problems that bedevilled our ever increasing flood of clients, and as the war came closer I could sympathise with the middle-class women who began to consult us.

Men in good positions were called to the army, where they earned fourteen shillings a week, seven shillings of which they had to allot to their wives, so that they were eligible to draw a dependant's allowance. These allowances were so pitifully small that they hardly paid the rent for many people. Women threatened suicide as they were increasingly bullied by hire purchase firms, mortgage companies or rent collectors because they could no longer pay. A few employers sent their employees' wives sufficient money to bring the allowance up to their husband's wages, but many, faced with profound changes in their businesses due to the war, were unable to do this. My colleague and I read up the laws on contracts till our eyes glazed and learned to find technicalities upon which we could break hire purchase agreements and so release our desperate clients. Finally, organisations such as ours were able to pressure the government into declaring a moratorium upon serving men's debts, and so keep the wolves from the door until the end of the war.

So experience poured in upon me – but at the back of my mind there was always the nagging thought that if I was ever to make progress in the world of social work, I would need that precious piece of paper, a degree. And I had not had the opportunity to matriculate.

On 1st September, all the lights of the city were turned off. It created a darkness which townsfolk had not faced before, and we blundered about like people suddenly blinded, and were touchingly grateful for a lighted match or the spark from the trolley of the electric trams to give us a bearing. At first we endured the blackout with shivery, laughing fortitude, but after a while it became a frustrating curse, a maddening tedium. It was dangerous, too, as traffic tried to move about in such dense darkness and pedestrians stumbled over unexpected steps and hazards, like the fire hydrants, wandering dogs and cats, and parked bicycles. I once walked into a letter box and went home with a streaming, bloody nose. We learned how beautiful the stars were and, until the bombing began, rejoiced in moonlit nights.

All schools were closed, because in principle all children were evacuated with their teachers. This meant that for the first time for years, I not only had no children to care for; I had no studying to do. All places of entertainment were also closed, with the exception of public houses which were small and had only a limited number of people gathered in them. I was accustomed to cramming my life with study, with house cleaning, with care of many of the children's needs and with tutoring in shorthand. My current shorthand student, a cripple, had been evacuated to Southport and I had not yet found a replacement, so although I worked long hours I sometimes found myself, late in the evening, sitting with Mother over a cup of tea, not knowing what to talk about. If I introduced a subject, I could never be sure that she would not take offence and begin one of her irrational rages, so I tended to sit in dismal silence, and leave her to talk if she wanted to. Her favourite subject was Father's backslidings or some incident in the office when she had bested an adversary. I felt sorry for the office.

Mother was herself undoubtedly at a loss. She was not in the least interested in me and, I think, endured my presence as best she could. Her usual retreat, the cinema, with its long programmes and two new films a week, was closed to her. She had no friends – I do not recollect her ever having a bosom friend, though in our palmier days she had many close acquaintances and admirers. Father sometimes asked if she would like to go with him to his favourite pub, 'Ye Hole in Ye Wall' in Hackins Hey, and have a drink. She would always respond tartly that, 'Ladies do not go into public houses.'

Looking back, I find it odd that neither of us at that point volunteered our help as wardens, telephonists, first aid personnel or anything else. Half the town was enrolled in some service or other, while we sat stiffly over our tea. For my part, I think it was both mental and physical exhaustion. Having to walk most of the distance to and from work and spend the day coping with other people's woes, many of them quandaries unheard of before, was a heavy strain. I rarely reached home before eight o'clock, a home where I still never had enough to eat. There was a limit to the number of the world's woes which I could take upon my skimpy shoulders.

In Mother's case it seemed as if there was a whole section of her which did not function at all. She never managed to bring any real order into her life, never mind into ours. The bright and intelligent mind, of which I sometimes caught a glimpse when she cared to talk about books, seemed to have been buried amid the wild, superficial gaiety of the post-war years and the disasters which had subsequently befallen us. Perhaps she was hopelessly drained, too.

So there she sat, drinking tea and popping aspirins into her mouth, while Poland was decimated and we waited for our turn.

Father bought two second-hand suitcases. The few spare clothes we had were packed into these, together with family papers, like birth certificates, marriage lines and army discharge papers. One case was kept by my parents' bed and one by mine, so that if the house caught fire from incendiary bombs, we could run outside with them. When the air raid siren went, we shot out of bed, grabbed our clothes and the cases and fled to the doubtful safety of the cellar steps. There were several false alarms at first, when the sirens howled, the anti-aircraft guns in the park rumbled, searchlights swung across the sky and part-time wardens ran along the streets, pushing everyone indoors. Still the bombers did not come.

We began to feel safer.

Mother bought some cheap dress material, striped in green and tan, and I stitched pretty covers, complete with shoulder straps, for our gas mask boxes. I also made each of us a matching turban and scarf. Mother, Fiona and I sailed out in these feeling very smart and up-to-date. After a while, like everyone else, we discovered what a convenient receptacle the gas mask box was. We left the gas masks at home and used the box to carry make-up, lunches and the inevitable cotton pocket handkerchief. When rationing commenced, Mother found that the ration books fitted very conveniently into hers.

With no student to tutor, I had very little money of my own. I not only walked to town, which was the first stage of my journey to work, I walked half way to Bootle as well, trudging a couple of miles along Scotland Road, a dreadfully poor area, and Stanley Road, to reduce the amount of the tram fare. I cut out lunch, except when there was enough bread in the house for me to take a slice of bread and margarine.

Rumours went about that one could earn huge sums in the new factories out at Speke, which were going into war production. I thought about this and then decided that after the war I could be out of work and walking the streets with hundreds of other unskilled workers. To become a qualified social worker as quickly as possible still seemed a good idea, if I could achieve it.

No one could complain to us that our work was not essential. Daily we filled an ever-widening gap between official mandates and the protesting, unhappy victims of them.

I missed very much my fellow typist, Miriam Enns. She lived too far away from me for us to meet socially, and anyway I had no money to pay for coffees in city tea shops, which would have been one way of seeing her. Gradually, I lost touch with her.

Sylvia Poole was working for a firm supplying medical aids, like bandages and cotton wool, and her company became very busy. We did, however, manage to go for prim little Sunday walks together, and, because of the slackened pressure in our house, Mother agreed that she should occasionally come to tea. Tea was a simple meal of bread and margarine and jam, followed by a cake bought from a shop which sold leftovers from a big bakery. Much to my delight, Sylvia and Mother got along famously, and Mother began to look forward to her coming, and would suggest that I ask her.

It was ironical that the commencement of a world war which threw the lives of millions into turmoil should at first give me a little more leisure. During the long walks home, I began to think of myself as a person in my own right and tiny independent wistful longings floated in the back of my mind. I had always had it drummed into me that I was a possession of my parents, to be moved around, fed or not fed, bullied or ignored, as they saw fit. I had fought against it instinctively for years, but I had always lost, excepting in regard to going to night school and obtaining my current job. Now, in little flashes, I began to wonder if one could not, after all, exist without somebody else's permission. But I was an exhausted bag of bones, worn out with years of intolerable strain, and the slave mentality which I had acquired was not going to be easily shed.

On Sunday, 3rd September, 1939, Father kept the radio on from early morning. He did not go for his usual walk. Mother and I went about our normal Sunday tasks of cleaning, cooking, washing and ironing, feeling particularly subdued. Even Fiona, who took little notice of anything which did not directly concern herself, got up earlier than usual, and wandered restlessly about the house, while we waited to see if Hitler would continue the war in Poland, despite the Allies' ultimatum. A tremendous, ominous silence lay over our old, black city as people stayed close to home. No children played in the street and no traffic passed along it. The old men who played ollies in the gutter did not come out for their customary game.

I read again a comforting letter which I had received from Friedrich the previous day. Our dear Fuehrer was apparently still uniting the German race and I was not to be afraid, just to keep on writing to his home address. Earlier in the week, I had received a hysterical letter from Ursel. Her husband, a minister, had been arrested for a sermon he had given defending the Jews, and she was terrified. How the letter got past the German censor is beyond me, unless they had become a little less efficient as a result of Germany's having to supervise so many newly acquired countries.

At eleven o'clock, we gathered in the living room to listen to the BBC. The tired voice of our Prime Minister, Mr Chamberlain, announced that we were at war. As we all stood up while the National Anthem boomed over the radio, we looked at each other. Mother and Father, veterans of that war to end all wars, Fiona, beautiful in spite of her hair curlers, a face as blank as the page of a new exercise book, and me with Friedrich's letter still in my pinafore pocket, all of us assured by our newspapers that we would be buried under the ruins of Liverpool within hours of the declaration of war. Would Friedrich be one of the bomber pilots, I wondered, fingering the gentle letter? Or was he at this moment too busy killing innocent Poles?

It seemed incredible, impossible. The weight on my chest was unbearable. I said in a grating voice, 'I think I'll make a cup of tea.'

Chapter nineteen

A few evenings later, mildly surprised, like everyone else, that I was still alive, I languidly hung up my coat in the hall, the same old brown coat so often pawned, now near the end of its days.

The door into the living room opened suddenly and I blinked in the light from the room's bare electric bulb. Fiona, with a piece of toast in one hand, stood in the doorway, and said with something like awe in her voice, 'Helen, you've got to go down to see the police.'

'What?'

She was obviously intrigued at this unexpected call for her eldest sister, and with a cheek swelled with toast, she repeated, 'You have! To see the police.'

Thoroughly alarmed, I forgot my hunger and hastened into the room. Father and Mother were seated at the table. They had just finished their evening meal, and thick white plates rimmed with bacon fat were scattered round the soiled cloth.

'Mother! What's wrong? I haven't done anything.'

Father answered me. 'Only Fiona had arrived home when they came. They left a message to say that you should go down to a place in Lime Street – and take with you any correspondence you had received from Germany.'

'Oh, my God!' I muttered. 'What would they want that for?'

Mother put her knife and fork neatly together on her plate. 'We don't know, Helen. We hope it isn't serious.'

'Am I supposed to go tonight?'

'It is nearly eight o'clock,' Father replied. 'They can wait. I'll take you down tomorrow evening. Try to get home early.'

Throughout the night I tossed sleeplessly, wracked by nervous fears. Had I broken the law in writing to Germany? Would they shut me up in an internment camp? Should I burn all the carefully kept letters and say I had none to show them? Friedrich had been courting me by mail. What would they say about that?

In the morning, as I washed myself in cold water in the kitchen, using a bit of Father's shaving soap since there was no other soap, and Father built the living room fire, I shouted to him to ask his advice. I made a clean, blushing admission of Friedrich's sentimental advances. As soon as I had my underclothes on, he came into the kitchen to wash his hands and get his razor. While I made Mother's early morning tea, he slowly lathered his face and thought about what I had said.

'We'll take the letters with us,' he finally decided. 'They will look so innocent – I am sure the police will understand. If you destroy them, they may become unduly suspicious – people do usually have some of the letters they receive, lying in drawers or desks.'

163

'O.K.,' I agreed reluctantly.

Because Father was a little behind in his shaving, I took Mother's tea up to her, and she broached the same subject as she huddled in the meagre bedding.

'Your Father and I were talking about your going to see the police. He says you must look nice. What are you doing about your clothes?'

Only twice before had Mother discussed clothes with me, at the time of my Confirmation and when she had helped me to buy the dress for the office dance. Now she sounded quite anxious.

I saw the point. A nicely dressed middle-class girl would be treated with greater respect.

'I hadn't thought about them. My coat is a mess, and I haven't needed a hat since the warmer weather started. No gloves. Social workers don't have to look smart, thank goodness. The turban and scarf I made for the spring don't look bad, though – I could wear those.'

Mother sipped her tea. 'Your Father is very worried. Could you buy a coat in your lunch hour? I have a pound that you can borrow.'

I was flabbergasted. I never looked for help from Mother – and now she was suddenly offering it. She *must* be worried. She earned very much more than I did, but I had not expected such a sudden change of mood.

'I could try, Mummy. C & A Modes might have something in their sale.'

'I don't think there is anything in the pawnbroker's which will fit.' Mother sipped the scalding hot, greyish brew thoughtfully.

Suddenly, I wanted a new coat passionately. I forgot about the police. I remembered only that I had never had a *new* overcoat since I was a child. 'I'll try, Mummy,' I said eagerly. 'I can pay you back bit by bit as soon as I get a new shorthand pupil – you'll remember that Miss Bennett was evacuated to Southport last week – but I have advertised for someone else.' I whistled under my breath. 'I'll have to go into town from Bootle, in my lunch hour. If I'm late back, the office will just have to put up with it for once.' I felt reckless in my longing for a coat.

At lunch time I had about ten minutes to find a garment at half-price in which to impress a suspicious police force, an impossible task.

Breathlessly, I looked through the racks of new stock – heavy winter coats just put on display – until a white-haired lady asked if she could help me. 'I've a pound to buy a coat,' I confessed frankly to her, and she was unexpectedly sympathetic. She suggested a lined mackintosh, and my face must have fallen, because she said, 'Come over to the back here. There are one or two items which were missed when we were putting away the summer stock after the sale yesterday.'

And there it was, a soft woollen coat, beige, with a narrow braid trim in orange and green round the collar. The top front button was missing, a loose thread marking where it should be.

'Try it on.'

I did. It fitted neatly on the shoulders and round a twenty inch waist. I twirled slightly, and the flared skirt swished round legs that I was astonished to see were slender and shapely. The turban, a hemmed length of tan cloth touched with green flecks, which I had made from a design in a magazine which Fiona had brought home, blended very well with the coat. The assistant tightened the belt slightly and stepped back.

I glowed, and inquired carefully, 'How much is it?'

'Nineteen shillings and eleven pence – marked down from thirty shillings.' She rubbed her chin thoughtfully, as she surveyed me. 'I think I can find you a similar button. The collar would nearly hide it, if it doesn't quite match.' She went to a table, opened a drawer and ran her fingers through an assortment of buttons and belts. She turned triumphantly with a beige button between her bright pink fingernails.

I apologised to my superior at the office for being five minutes late, and plunged into work. Later when a moment of calm arrived and I had made a cup of tea for both of us, I told her that I had to go with my father that evening on some special family business and asked if I could leave promptly.

She sighed and the weary lines under her eyes deepened. 'Of course,' she said. She was only about seven or eight years older than myself, and I wondered suddenly if our clients were worth the sacrifices she made for them. Since leaving university, she had given all her young days to them, given them her life, working far into the evenings and at weekends to try to find help for them. And I wanted to do the same thing. Or did I?

Father had to pay my tram fares into the city, because I had spent my last travel money for that week on the additional trip going to and from the dress shop. In a brown paper bag lay practically all Friedrich's letters and most of Ursel's passionate epistles, including the last terrified cry. The pride in the new coat had gone and had been replaced by feelings akin to panic.

Father was grave and, at first, silent. On the tram, he murmured to me to answer any questions put to me, and then he qualified the remark by adding, 'And don't say anything more than that. I will introduce us.'

We were passed from a uniformed constable, to a sergeant and then to a plain-clothes policeman, as we worked our way into the bowels of a building in Lime Street. This was not the police station – it bore all the marks of makeshift offices hastily set up. Father had assumed like an overcoat the quiet air of authority and the cultivated language of the public school man that he was, and this outweighed his cheap clothes, and had its effect. The higher one was in the social heirarchy the more carefully the police handled one.

Finally, we were seated at a small table sheltered by a cloth screen, which looked as if it might have started life in a hospital fifty years before. The room was a large one, containing a number of tables similarly set up, and men and women sat round them whispering and shuffling papers, like relations going through desks after a funeral. I stared up at a high ceiling, finely moulded as if for a ballroom, but covered with dust and drooping spiders' webs. Pale green walls were discoloured from ancient water leakages and the passage of many people.

Two new plain-clothes men joined us. One sat opposite me at the table, the other one perched on a stool slightly at a distance half behind me. Nervous as a new climber faced with a precipice, I clenched my hands on my lap and braced myself for whatever might come.

It was an ordeal. The fear of internment, perhaps imprisonment, haunted me, though at no point was either mentioned by my interrogators. At times I thought I would surely faint before it was over.

Once our relationship and our names were established, Father sat quietly. I produced the letters and laid them in two neat piles before the man at the table. He was middle-aged, with deep lines criss-crossing a craggy face. Small, hard blue eyes glittered between reddish-gold eyelashes. Thin, tightly curled hair had been plastered down each side of his head with a heavy application of strongly scented pomade, an odour combined with the heavy smell of stale cigarette smoke. He and the man behind me smoked incessantly, and the pile of cigarette butts rose in a dirty white saucer on the table. I was offered a cigarette, but whispered that I did not smoke. A battered packet of Player's was offered to Father, and he took one and smoked it slowly, while he listened.

A young man in a shabby blue suit had pulled another chair forward and sat down. He had brought with him a small pile of writing paper, some folders and a couple of well-sharpened yellow pencils. He had arranged a shorthand notebook on his knee and was taking notes of everything that was said. This threw me into further alarm. I shifted myself fractionally, so that I could see what the young man wrote. My own shorthand was first class and I had often transcribed from the other typists' work. I had no difficulty in reading what he wrote, even at an odd angle. If he doesn't get it down correctly, I will correct him, I promised myself, like a terrier prepared to defend its territory from a Great Dane, all bombast and no clout.

Age? Place of birth? All the addresses I had ever lived at – Father had to aid my memory about this one. Jobs? Schools? My short time at school was explained by Father as being because of Mother's bad health – but these were not school officials, they were detectives. Religious affiliation? Friends?

Friends? Had I really only two? Miriam and Sylvia? Boy friends? Only Friedrich? Was I sure? No casual men friends that I met only occasionally?

'No,' I snapped indignantly. 'I'm too busy.' Why could not they see that that was a stupid question to a girl who looked like me?

'Why did you study German?'

I looked at him dumbly. Why did one study anything? Because one wanted to know.

'I wanted to make up my lack of ordinary education,' I told my grim interrogator cautiously.

'Most people learn French.'

'I am learning French as well.'

'Humph.'

We sat silent for a moment, looking at each other. The blue eyes were cold and hard, mine a little moist because I felt physically weak and helpless. Why were they bothering me like this? I wanted to ask. But

Father had warned me only to answer questions, not to ask them.

I half closed my eyes, so that the detective should not see the tears threatening. Under my lids I took a quick look at the shorthand writer's notebook. On his current page, the record was correct, right down to the exact wording of Father's interjection about my schooling.

The detective was reading Friedrich's letters. Apparently he read German easily and was flicking from one page to another quickly.

'How did you come into contact with Friedrich Reinhardt?'

I half smiled. I was immediately whisked into a train lumbering northwards towards Crewe. I was travelling alone, as usual, on my annual visit to Grandma's. On the window seat next to me sat a boy about two years older than me. He was dressed in a grown up suit of unusual cut, rather shabby. He was slim, hair dark and slightly wavy, with a heart-shaped face and a flawless white skin.

The train was a local one which stopped at almost every station, and at each stop the boy would peer anxiously out of the window. Two adults in the compartment, a middle-aged husband and wife, had, after staring at both of us, opened newspapers and retired behind them.

Very shyly, the boy had turned to me and asked, 'Pardon me. Where are you travelling?' His accent was foreign.

Equally shyly, I had peeped up from under the brim of my panama school hat, and whispered,

'Liverpool,' as if it were important that the other travellers did not hear me.

'I must the train at Crewe leave. A man comes for me there.'

'I change at Crewe. I will tell you when we arrive.'

'Much thanks.' He relaxed his vigil of station watching, and I sat the doll I had been nursing down on the seat beside me and arranged its skirts modestly. He smiled at it, rather patronisingly, and I smiled at him. Boys never understood what a friend a doll could be.

It was the beginning of a long friendship, all of two hours. I left with a note of his address and the promise to write. It was a simple address, the name of a village near Munich. Neither of us did write, of course, and the slip of paper was lost before I returned from Grandma's. But the address was not lost. It stayed in my mind with the picture of a beautiful youth and a lovely train journey through the green Midlands of England. When I began to learn German and the class was encouraged by the teacher to find a German pen-friend, I had remembered it like a nursery rhyme and all the other odds and ends which children keep in a mental rag bag.

'How did you get the name and address of Reinhardt in order to write to him?'

I jumped at the sharp repetition of the question. The granite face before me was formidable. I told him.

'You have a remarkable memory.' The tone was heavily sarcastic.

'Children remember all kinds of things,' I responded woodenly.

171

'What was he doing in England?'

'He was going to stay with English friends of his father's – friends from long ago before the war – to improve his English. It was already quite good. He could talk about almost anything – but not correctly.'

'Where was he going?'

'To Manchester.'

'And where had he come from?'

I was getting fed up and snapped back, 'I didn't ask him.' Father cleared his throat reprovingly.

I thought I was being grilled thoroughly but when, after what seemed hours, we finally got down to Ursel's letters, questions about Friedrich seemed nothing.

I had been put into touch with Ursel when I had replied to a letter in the Sunday *Observer*, which Father had once bought. The letter offered to put children in touch with pen-friends in Germany. I had asked for a girl friend. The detective told me that my letter of so many years earlier had been found by the police in the file of the man who wrote the letter to the *Observer*, a known Fascist.

I stared at the detective unbelievingly. 'Who on earth would bother to retain such a letter? And why are you interested in such a silly thing as two girls writing to each other?'

The detective did not answer. He was reading one of Ursel's letters. Perhaps he did not like his work being considered silly.

Then he launched his attack. Question after question. Small things that Ursel had asked about, matters

I had long since forgotten. How had I replied? What did this paragraph or that one refer to? Questions until I was dizzy and bewildered. Finally, Father intervened to remind the detective reproachfully that I was only a young girl.

'Twenty is not a young girl,' retorted the detective tartly. 'Please be quiet. I have my work to do.'

Father was obviously getting very upset. But he did keep quiet.

Nine o'clock. Ten o'clock by the timepiece on the wall. I began to think we would never be allowed to go home. And I still did not understand what all the fuss was about. I was floundering in bewilderment.

At about eleven, it came suddenly to an end. The man who had been sitting quietly nearly behind me, said, 'I think that will do, Tom.' He swung his heavy body round to look at me. 'We will have a summary typed up. You can sign it and then you can go. If you change your address you must let us know immediately.'

The curly-headed detective stood up and stretched himself. Unexpectedly, he asked quite pleasantly, 'Would you like a cup of tea?' He picked up Friedrich's and Ursel's letters, shuffled them into a neat pile and put them into a folder handed him by the stenographer.

I nodded silently. Father said, 'Thank you.'

The three men went away, and I turned to Father, 'What ... ?' I began in a quavery voice.

Father said very softly, 'Don't say anything.' He made the smallest possible gesture towards the screen half-surrounding us, and mouthed, 'Listening.'

I swallowed, and said in a normal voice. 'I hope they bring the tea.' If they were listening, they might as well be reminded of their promise. Then I sat with hands crossed on my lap, like a tabby kitten tired of play, and watched people coming and going through the door.

After a little while, a bald-headed elderly constable in uniform brought two cups of tea, with Marie biscuits tucked into the saucers. 'There you are, Miss, Sir,' he said politely, as he put the cups down on the table.

We ate the biscuits and drank the tea in perfect silence, while we listened to the rise and fall of innumerable muffled conversations in the huge room. Men in uniform, men in civilian clothes, occasionally women of various ages and classes, were ushered through. How late did the police work? I wondered.

At five to twelve, the curly-headed detective returned, bearing several sheets of closely-typed paper. 'Sorry you had to wait so long,' he said quite cheerfully, and plunked himself down on his chair once more. He started to read the closely-typed sheets very carefully, running his forefinger along each line. I noticed that he had lost his little finger and I sat watching the slight movement of the stub as the non-existent finger tried to adjust to the movement of the others.

The stenographer and the second detective joined us at the table, their faces looking nearly as rumpled as their navy blue suits.

The summary of the conversation was handed to me, with the request to read it and sign it.

Father uncrossed his legs and leaned towards me. For the first time he looked tense.

'Read it very carefully, Helen. If for any reason you feel it deviates from what was said, I am sure the officer will have it altered.'

The officer sighed and looked at his watch. He blew through his lips, making a soft pooh-poohing sound, and then agreed, 'Yes, it can be altered.'

I was no lawyer but I was used to reading contracts, new laws and government directives and interpreting them to our clients. The stenographer had composed a very fair summary of what had transpired. A lawyer, no doubt, would have queried every sentence, but I did not have such an adviser. In fact, it never occurred to Father or me that we could have demanded the presence of a lawyer, though I cannot imagine how we would have managed to pay him anyway.

I borrowed Father's fountain pen, and signed.

Chapter twenty

The signature had a galvanising effect. The stenographer, hovering in the background, was dismissed. The detective who had been the observer at the interview seized a weather-beaten trilby from an old-fashioned hat stand nearby, clapped it on his head, said 'Good night,' to us, and 'See you in the morning, Tom,' to my diligent questioner, and fled after the stenographer.

The big room seemed suddenly nearly deserted. Tom leaned back in his chair and stretched himself. He rubbed his eyes and grinned like a schoolboy at Father and me. The rocklike hardness of his expression vanished completely and we were faced with an average Liverpudlian, who might have been a small businessman of some kind.

'How are you going to get home?' he asked Father.

Father did not have a watch, so I looked at Grandma's watch and said to Father, 'It's half past twelve. We shall have to walk.'

Father rose and nodded to the detective.

'Like to wait a few minutes? I'll drop you in my car.'

Father was looking completely worn out and both of us had to be up by six the next morning, so I smiled impulsively at the detective, and said, 'That would be lovely.'

The detective gazed slyly at me through red eye-lashes. 'Forgiven?' he asked.

My smile died. 'You have to do your work,' I replied. 'But I wish you'd tell us what it is all about.'

He stood up, moved around the table and then perched himself on the edge of it, facing Father. 'Well, I can tell you this. Your daughter is not what we are looking for. We are quite satisfied about that.' He stopped, and again blew his soft pooh-poohing sound. 'We're checking everyone known to have any association with Germany. We could have a Fifth Column here, ready to betray us – you must realise that. Your daughter's letter about a pen-friend was found in the files of a known Nazi, when we picked him up. He had a neat little espionage system going, you know. Linked up children in one district in England with a single class in a German school.'

I gasped, and he grinned at me.

'The English letters addressed to one school in Germany were read by German intelligence before delivery.' He paused, and shrugged. 'You can appreciate how it would work. Kids write about where they live and what their father does for a living – whether he has been called up or sent to work in a new factory. Undoubtedly, questions were suggested to the German children for them to ask their pen-friends; I've checked enough piles of correspondence like Helen's to realise this. If they had enough letters they would get a very good picture of what was going on in a given town in England – and Liverpool, being a big port, would be of particular interest.'

'Good Lord!' exclaimed Father. 'You mean that Helen had actually become part of this?'

'Yes.' He turned and grinned down at me. 'But her pen-friend had left school early to be married. I gathered from her letters that she was married at sixteen?'

'She was,' I agreed sadly. 'She was terribly unhappy. Her husband was a Minister in her church – and he was nearly forty.'

'So, you see, she could not be prompted in her questions – without telling her how she was being used. And from her last letter I gather that her husband was in deep trouble with the Nazis.'

I sighed, and nodded agreement.

'But why put me through all this . . . ?' I gestured helplessly.

'Had to be certain, my dear. And you work in a place where many of the staff are highly politically minded.'

Dumbfounded, I stared at him. I thought of Miriam and her high ideals – and then I remembered that, only the month before, Russia had signed a non-aggression pact with Germany. I whistled under my breath, an unladylike habit learned as a child from a shepherd.

'From Communists, Conchies, Catholics and Cranks, good Lord deliver us,' the detective was saying to Father. He glanced again at me, sitting frightened in my chair. 'What's a pretty little thing like you doing, working in a place like that? You should be out enjoying yourself – dancing.'

I was deeply offended and said loyally through

gritted teeth, 'The ladies I work with do a wonderful job. I sometimes think they prevent this city from bursting into riots from sheer misery. At least people can talk to us about their troubles.'

His red eyebrows shot up and he made a face. 'Well . . .' He swung off the table, and abruptly changed the subject. 'I'll get the car. You know your way to the front door?'

We agreed that we did, and we stole down quiet corridors where lights still burned behind closed doors, to wait in front of the building.

At first, after the light inside the building, we faced a wall of complete darkness, but gradually our eyes became accustomed to it. Familiar Lime Street began to emerge. The outline of St George's Hall loomed against the sky in front of us. Intermittent flashes from the shaded lights of cars lit up for a moment the squat block of the War Memorial or the finely-cast fish whose tails held up the lamp-standards. Other than the occasional sound of a car engine the busy city was absolutely quiet, and I jumped violently when above my head a sleepy pigeon cooed once.

'I'm glad we don't have to walk home in such darkness,' I remarked to Father. I was deeply angry at the detective's derisory remarks, but the safety of his car would be welcome.

'I should buy a torch,' replied Father, 'and you should get one, too.'

I shrugged. When would I be able to afford a torch? I wondered suddenly if Father knew that Mother received practically all my salary, and that to all intents and purposes I worked for nothing.

'Could you lend me fourpence for my fares tomorrow?' I inquired hopefully. 'Now I'm out at Bootle, it is too far for me to walk. I'll pay you back as soon as I get a student.'

'I can,' Father replied. 'I won't have to pay our fares back tonight, thanks to friend Tom.'

A small car swooshed around the corner and drew up at the kerb. We felt our way carefully down the steps. The door was opened from within and the front seat tipped forward, so that I could clamber into the back seat. Father sat by Tom, and as we swept through the empty streets, they talked fitfully about the invasion of Poland by the Germans and the sinking of the *Athenia* by German submarines.

When we stopped in our deserted street, I leaned forward and asked, 'May I have my letters back sometime, if I come for them?'

Tom laughed. 'Not till the end of the war, luv – round Christmas, probably. They have to stay in our files until it's over.'

'That's not quite fair, is it? You said I wasn't what you were looking for.'

'Can't be helped, luv.' He turned round to look at me over his shoulder. 'You should forget about your German boy friend. Find yourself a nice English lad.'

I drew in my breath crossly. I resented Friedrich being termed a boy friend. It seemed to belittle him. But one does not argue with the police. Father had got out of the car and was holding the front seat forward for me. I slid out as gracefully as I could, and paused for a second to shake my skirts straight again.

The detective leaned across the front seat towards

us. I saw the flash of his teeth as he grinned. 'Remember what I said, young lady. Cranks, Conchies, Communists and Catholics – get out of it. Enjoy yourself while you're young.'

I seethed with anger. Father bent and shut the door, after saying good night and thanking the man for the lift.

'The abominable bigot!' I exclaimed furiously to Father, as he felt around in his pocket for the house key. 'I had no idea police could be so narrow minded. I could cheerfully have shot him.'

Father sighed. 'They are like the rest of us.'

Father had been so good about coming with me to the interview, that I did not want to argue with him, so I swallowed my flaring temper and did not answer him.

The letters never were returned to me. They probably still lie in some dusty crate of war-time files of the CID, a gentle record of innocent young people touching each others' lives across a mighty gulf.

Chapter twenty-one

'Mummy, I haven't got enough clothes,' wailed Fiona, oblivious of small matters like a full-scale war. 'I can't wear this dress *again*, going out with Reg.'

So Mother retrieved some bundles from pawn. Since they contained all kinds of garments, I benefited by the addition of a summer dress and a blouse to my small wardrobe. Both Mother and Fiona were considerably plumper than I was and these garments were too tight for them. This did not stop them 'borrowing' them – and anything else of mine left clean and folded on the shelf in our bedroom. The resultant burst under-arm seams were left for me to repair, which I did with savagely bad temper. I had also to wash and iron the garments.

When I turned on her in anger, Fiona would say mildly, 'But your things are always ready. I don't have time to see to my clothes.' And it was with difficulty that I refrained from hitting her.

Mother always helped herself, with the remark that I was welcome to borrow anything of hers. But she, like Fiona, rarely washed or pressed her clothes until she had nothing fresh left to wear. Anyway, both Fiona's and her clothes hung on my wasted frame.

The absence of the children and Alan considerably eased the financial strain. Mother's excellent salary meant that there was a little more food in the house, though frequently it was not the most nutritious kind. I still lacked lunch quite often, but a proper, though modest, breakfast helped me through the day, and there was a little more on my plate at night. There was far less work to do at home, no studying and no student to teach, so the awful strain on me began to slacken, despite long hours of work and travel. Yet I was totally miserable.

One weekend, Mother brought home some cheap wallpaper with a garish pattern of bright red cherries and green leaves printed all over it, and we covered the dingy grey walls of the living room with it. Emboldened by the improvement, Mother bought some cotton curtaining in similar colours, but emblazoned with roses, and we stitched curtains and, also, padded seat covers for the upended paint cans which formed some of our seating. The effect was very cheerful.

We still lacked sufficient bedding and sheets, and as the autumn crept on the increasing cold began to make my legs ache abominably. The bedding from the boys' beds had been pawned the day they were evacuated.

A general boredom set in as the fear of being bombed to death receded. I spent some weekend evenings with Mrs Poole and Sylvia. Mrs Poole, a professional dressmaker, showed me the proper way to cut out and fit a dress. But I could not afford to buy any material.

It seemed that nobody was interested in learning shorthand in such uncertain times. A small advertisement in the *Liverpool Echo*, paid for with the last fee of my evacuated student, brought no result.

Despite my anger at the derogatory remarks of the detective, he had sparked in me the idea of looking elsewhere for a better paying job, and I began to scan the Situations Vacant columns of the *Echo*. I wanted a position in which I could use my burgeoning experience in social work. I did not particularly want to be a secretary, for which type of position I was quite well qualified, unless it could be to a private person. There were still a few people in those days who had live-in secretaries, and in a big private house I felt that to a degree I could return to the kind of life which I had known in childhood. I wrote in reply to several such advertisements and received one response from Chester. An interview was arranged in the Adelphi Hotel. I did not get the job. My poor clothes, despite the new overcoat, and my generally neglected and unhealthy looks, together with a gauche, painfully shy manner, made it certain that I would never obtain a post in a private house. A more cultivated and presentable young woman would be essential.

With time to think, my inadequacies became even more painfully apparent to me. Yet I seemed shut into a situation of such acute penury that it was impossible to alter myself very much, and I cried myself to sleep a number of nights.

I had never discussed the situation at home with Sylvia. I shrank from trying to explain to anyone the hardships we had been enduring and the weird, bewildered lostness of my parents. Much of the time they seemed to float in a mist through which they were incapable of finding their way, though, as I pondered, I realised that Father had been trying recently to reach out to his children. Looking back, it is clear that Sylvia and I rarely discussed our personal feelings or our emotional life. We fed each other with talks about political events, books, theatres, history – a lively intellectual stimulation, almost bereft of the giggles and gossip of ordinary youngsters. Perhaps Sylvia had other friends who fulfilled this youthful need, but I did not.

There was no one to whom I could confide my shy desire to look chic, to learn to behave appropriately, become a normal middle-class girl again, groomed and cared for. Even the working-class girls who lived round me knew how to take care of their hair and their skin.

Wistfully I thought that if I had a little money to spend on pins and setting lotions, Fiona would show me how to do my hair. Mother spent a lot of time showing Fiona how to use hair tints and face creams and make-up. She bought her a fair amount of clothing and all this, added to a natural beauty, made her stunning to look at. All she had to do was smile in a lift or in the café where she had her lunch and it did not take long for well-heeled young men working in the city to find a polite way of approaching her and making a date. She was introduced by them into a circle of young people where she was accepted and was invited to parties, balls and dances. She soon learned from the more refined girls that she met how to deport herself, and this, added to her normal gentleness, made her quite popular amongst them. She sometimes amused me in bed by telling me of small incidents that indicated that she had succeeded where I had failed; she was on an upwardly mobile path. I wondered if I would ever learn to put a teacup down on a table without upsetting it, enter a room without tripping over the rug, the small social etiquette of when to take off gloves and hat, when to shake hands and when to greet a girl with a kiss; such small things, yet so important in a world still ruled by etiquette.

At twenty I was still wearing the glasses bought for me ten years before. The frames were hopelessly small and had not been improved by several poor repairs. A few years later much of my clumsiness disappeared when I was able to buy a new pair and see properly again.

But I had no money for hairpins, never mind expensive things like spectacles, and now no money for make-up or lunches or even stockings. Few people in those days had the courage to ask an employer for an increase in pay, and I lacked the courage of a mouse. My fear of unemployment had been enhanced by the lack of response to my tentative efforts to obtain another post. And I still owed Mother the pound she had lent me for the coat, about which she had reminded me caustically only a week before.

The visiting of clients in their homes, which I had been doing since my transfer to the Bootle office, had taught me that, though many of them were in dire straits, a great number of them lived far more comfortably than we did. They were simply better managers. Strangely, the war had not made much difference to the number of unemployed, but increasingly they seemed to be finding ways of earning small sums to augment their parish relief. They talked quite frankly to me about these little jobs, trusting me not to make a record of the information. If I had reported them, any money they earned would have immediately been deducted from their meagre allowance from the Relieving Officer. The women cleaned the homes of the more prosperous, the men did gardening, worked as handymen and sometimes as casual labour on building sites. No matter what time I called, there usually seemed to be a fire in the grate. What they most suffered from was overcrowding in dilapidated, verminous houses, lack of bathrooms, hot water and indoor lavatories, things that they could not themselves do a great deal about. Their rents were controlled at such a low level that it was in many cases impossible for landlords to find the money for repairs, renovations or fumigation.

At home, we never learned to manage so successfully.

One Saturday, after a visit to a client, I had to spend twopence in a public telephone box to check something for the woman concerned, with my superior in the office. Afterwards I was in great distress when I realised that, though I would have the twopence returned to me eventually, I now had no money to pay my fare back to the centre of the city. I would have to walk there, and then the rest of the way from the city centre up the hill to our house. I was already sorely troubled that I had no fares left for the following week also.

I thought I would never reach home as I trudged along Stanley Road. I was dreadfully tired and still badly undernourished. At St Luke's Church, I sat

187

down on the steps because I felt I could go no further. People passing glanced at me curiously, so I shut my eyes until the world had stopped swimming around me.

It was a mild day, sunny enough for the rays to fight their way through the cloud of pollutants that veiled Liverpool on the few days when it was not windy. I should be able to manage four or five miles, I told myself, now that the situation at home had eased.

Jumbled, chaotic thoughts wandered through a dulled mind, as I sat trying to get my breath. The detective had suggested that I should enjoy myself, go dancing. He must have been crazy. Things like that cost money. Even to volunteer, say, as a part-time air raid warden, which would have given me new friends, would need a few more pennies for fares, for the odd cup of coffee, possibly for uniform. Eyes still closed I put my head down on my handbag on my knee, and laughed.

'Are ye all right, luv?'

An elderly newspaper seller had shuffled across the road and was bending over me solicitously. I looked up, startled. Small kind eyes stared at me through cheap metal-framed glasses balanced on a bulbous red nose.

'Yes, thank you. Yes. I had to rest a moment, that's all.'

'Thought you was goin' to faint.'

I smiled up at him. 'No. I'm fine now, thank you very much.'

He grinned and toddled back to his little table of newspapers.

With gritted teeth I made myself climb the hill.

At the Rialto, leaning one trench-coated shoulder against a stucco pillar, lounged the pimp who had once offered me a cigarette. I wondered if his girls felt much worse than I did. He said good night as he always did, tipping his rakish trilby hat as he did so. He must have found me rather a joke, because I looked so prim, yet despite his despicable occupation, I always smiled and replied politely, 'Good night.'

This night I was almost shaky enough to ask him for a cigarette, to quell my hunger and soothe the great tide of unhappiness which was threatening to engulf me. It beat in my head, choked my throat. Years and years of suppressed misery welled up; thoughts of all my lost girlhood, all the possibly happy, irresponsible years lost in grinding poverty and an incredible weight of work, marched past me and jeered at me, as if to say, 'You think you were *entitled* to live and laugh and be happy? Don't kid yourself. You've got years and years of semi-slavery before you – and nothing much else.'

The house was incredibly quiet as I entered. I shivered. Without the children, I felt bereft of a reason for living.

Father and Mother sat on either side of the fire-place reading the paper. For once, they were not quarrelling. The puppy recently brought home by Brian slumbered unheeding on the coconut matting, his back braced against the warm fender, the current stray cat curled comfortably on top of him. It was a great friendship. Fiona must long since have gone out with a date.

Both parents looked up and said, 'Hello.'

I responded with a small, tight 'hello' back, and went straight to the kitchen to fill the kettle at the sink. When I twisted a knob on the gas stove, gas hissed out of one of the rings and I thankfully lit a match and put it to the ring. I could make tea quickly.

There was a slice of commercially cooked ham on a plate in the kitchen, and I called, 'Is the ham for me?' My voice sounded as if I were being strangled.

'Yes,' Mother called back, and I heard the rustle of the newspaper as she turned the page, and it grated on my raw nerves. I took two pieces of bread from a packaged sliced loaf, dabbed some margarine on them and put the ham between them. When the kettle boiled, I asked Mother and Father if they would like tea; if so, I would make a full pot. They both decided to have some.

With agitated hands, cups were somehow rinsed under the cold water from the tap and assembled on the table with the ham sandwich. I sat down in front of them and looked at them. My throat felt tight to choking point. Within there was a rising feeling of panic. In a minute, I thought frantically, I am going to scream – and scream – about nothing.

That was it. Scream about nothing. Scream about the void which was me. About a non-existent person, with no meaning to anyone else but me – or perhaps Sylvia. My God, how I wished she was there.

Moving like a zombie, I poured and distributed the tea. I bit at the sandwich and rolled the cottonwool bread with its stringy piece of ham round my mouth.

I chewed, but could not swallow it, trying all the time to control the irrational hysteria rising in me.

I took a big breath, then sipped some tea to help the sandwich down. I choked.

Hand to mouth, I fled to the kitchen sink and succeeded in spitting out the offending piece of sandwich. I began to cry.

It was as if a well-locked lid had suddenly burst from a gas tank, because of uncontrollable pressure from within. I could hear myself groaning and screaming, as I clung to the edge of the sandstone sink, frightful primitive cries of a creature beyond help, writhing as if in pain.

Pain it was. All the pain, all the suppressed grief of nine dreadful years, coming to the surface, now that some of the intense load had been lifted, the revolt of a human creature nearly pressed out of existence. Screams of awful mental anguish.

Chapter twenty-two

In a flurry of dropped newspapers, Mother and Father were beside me in a second.

'Good God, Helen! Whatever's the matter?' Father's face was shocked.

But I could not answer. I was far away, outside the tortured being standing at the sink, totally unable to take command again of my normal territory. I shrieked like an air raid siren out of control.

Mother took my arm and shook me. 'Stop it, Helen! Do you hurt somewhere?'

Hurt? I hurt all over. The shrieks became wild laughter.

Father seized me by the shoulders, turned me towards him and administered a great slap across my face.

It was partially effective. Mind and body snapped together again. With a hand to my stinging face, I continued to cry helplessly, bellowing like Avril in a tantrum. But I no longer laughed or shrieked. And this was no trantrum. It was like the cries of someone just bereaved. Mother put her arm round me and led me into the living room. 'Sit down,' she ordered, and parked me on a straight chair by the table. I laid my head on the table and continued to cry helplessly. 'Tell us what is the matter.' Her voice was unexpectedly concerned, and somehow the unusual tone caused greater paroxysms of tears.

Father, standing anxiously beside me, produced his dismally grey pocket handkerchief, and proffered it. I took it and wept into it.

Mother pulled up another straight chair and sat down. 'Are you ill?'

I nodded negatively. I could not put into words what ailed me. How can you say to the person most responsible that you are broken-hearted?

'Perhaps you'd feel better if you lay down for a little while,' suggested Father. In the Victorian and Edwardian world from which he came, women were entitled to have the vapours, a tearful manifestation of low spirits. They were usually persuaded to lie down and have smelling salts and brandy administered to them, until they could rise and face their terribly narrow world again. The connection struck me immediately and caused fresh storms of sobs.

'Nervous breakdown?' Mother whispered to Father, and I wanted to scream again.

'I hope to God not,' replied Father, as if I was not there. And that was the root of the trouble. To both of them most of the time I was not there – I did not exist. I rubbed my face on the dirty cloth and howled.

Mother patted the back of my head. 'I think bed is best. Come along upstairs, and when you are rested you can tell us what the trouble is.'

I was too far gone to care what happened, so I was led upstairs, kicked off my shoes and lay down on my bed. Mother brought a blanket to cover me, as I continued to cry. It was as if I would never be able to stop.

Father sat on the edge of the bed, while Mother went to fill Edward's hot water bottle.

'What's the matter, old lady?' Father asked, while Mother was downstairs

'It's all too much,' I nearly shrieked. 'I'm so tired. So tired and so lonely. I work hard – I never stop – and I never get anywhere.' I wept on, while Father sat, quiet, on the bed.

'I feel so weak – and I'm always hungry. And I've no money to buy anything at all – and I wonder if I ever will have. And nobody seems to notice or care. Nobody cares a tinker's cuss.'

I turned on my face and roared into my knobbly pillow.

Father caught one flaying hand in his own tiny hands, which went white at the slightest cold because his heart was so bad.

'Don't say, that, dear,' he responded, as if hurt to the quick. 'You're my Helen Rose. I care.' He started to unclench my fist and to rub my hand as if it were cold. 'Things are much better than they were, dear.'

'They are for everybody else,' I wailed, 'Not for me.' He continued to rub my hand. 'I wish I was dead,' I raved.

Mother came in with the hot water bottle. I took it from her and put it instinctively to my stomach, where the pain usually was, and curled up round it in a foetal position. I began to hold Father's hand as if it were a lifeline.

The room was nearly dark, so Mother lit a candle and put it on the mantelpiece. Then she, too, sat on the edge of the bed. There was silence, except for the sound of my weeping. The concern of both parents was undoubted, but in a corner of my mind which was beginning to function it appeared to me that it was the fear of the scandal of mental illness, rather than concern for me as a person, which bothered them. Probably this was unfair, but such was the distrust built into me since infancy.

I do not know for how long I cried. The storm began gradually to retreat, until I was sobbing occasionally, eyes sealed tight. The warmth of the blanket and the hot water bottle began to relax me, and I lay exhausted.

I lay quite still, too drained and fatigued to speak. Father still patiently held my hand, waiting for me to recover. Mother began to fidget round the room. 'Feeling better?' she inquired.

I looked dully at her silhouette against the candle. 'Yes, thank you,' I muttered, and then added hesitantly, 'I'm sorry.'

'That's all right, dear. You rest now. I'm going to attend to the blackout, and then I'll make some fresh tea and bring it up.' She turned briskly to Father, and said, 'You had better stay with her.'

'Of course,' Father assured her, and gave my hand a little squeeze. He must have been getting cramp from my holding on to his hand for so long, but I felt that if I let go, and lost the human contact, I would slip back again into hysteria.

I heard the big shutters in the living room being slammed and the iron bar being threaded across them, and then the ting of the rings on the blackout curtains which we had so painstakingly hand stitched; there were small thuds as Mother put some books along their hems to hold them flat against the window, so that light did not seep through. I began to cry again. The thought of the war made me feel even more helpless.

Father carefully put my hand down. 'I'll blow the candle out – the Warden may spot it.' He went over and blew out the small flame, and the odour of the smoking wick permeated the room. I watched him, still sobbing. He turned and looked out of the window through which the faint last afterglow of the sunset filtered. Over the chimneys of the houses huddled close to the back of our home, the thin, pencil line of a searchlight swept slowly across the sky.

Between huge, shuddering sobs, I said, 'I'm sorry to make such a fuss, Daddy.'

He turned and came slowly back to me. Seated on the bed, he faced me and asked, 'What happened?'

I tried to compose myself, and in unhappy gasps, I answered, 'It's nothing really, Daddy. I'm stupid. I spent my return fare from the office on a telephone call for a client. So I had to walk home from Bootle – and it seemed the last straw. I'm so tired – I feel I want to die with it.'

'You've had a lot of illness, I know. But I thought you were quite well.'

'I suppose I am.' Still weeping, I pulled myself up to a sitting position.

He sat looking anxiously at me, while I tried, not very successfully, to control myself.

'It wasn't exactly being without the twopence to

come back to the city – it was the whole thing. Every-body in the family – all their needs – seem to be con-sidered – but never me. I haven't a penny. I can't find another student to teach. No lunch, no make-up, no clothes. I'm desperate for new stockings.' My voice rose with a hint of hysteria again. 'If it wasn't for the Greek gentleman who gave us theatre money again this winter, I would never have been able to do anything. Even to visit Sylvia costs tram fares.'

'Have you told your mother?'

'Oh, Daddy! Ever since I went to work, she has done her best to make it impossible for me to stay there. She wants me home as a cheap housekeeper. She wouldn't give me a penny.' I put my head in my hands and cried some more.

'She paid for a coat for you recently.'

'She *lent* me the money – and she wants it back.' I nearly screamed in fury, 'And I only got that in the hope of not having the police on our backs – that would have been a real scandal, wouldn't it? Nice families don't get called in by the police, do they?' I put my head on my knees and lamented like a wind on the moors.

Father put his arms around me, the first time I ever remember him doing so, and did his best to comfort me.

A very subdued Mother brought me tea, which I drank. Then as my sobs subsided, she suggested that I try to sleep. Still shuddering, I thanked them both and obediently lay down like an exhausted rabbit in a thorn bush.

Chapter twenty-three

Through my troubled sleep, I was aware of a first-class uproar in the living room below. The battle between Mother and Father was joined again while I lay in bed on Sunday morning – the first Sunday I ever remember staying in bed, except when I had been ill.

Shattered and demoralised, I lay by Fiona, crying softly and listening to the enraged voices going back and forth. I wondered if I was indeed losing my reason.

A little more food had come my way. We had a fire more often, and usually there were enough pennies to provide a minimum of gas and electricity. These were solid gains, for which I should be grateful. I did not realise that it is not the actually starving who revolt – they are too weak – rather, it is the underfed, the underprivileged, who feel that the system could provide more for them. My system – my family – had taken my money, my work, my affection – and had given very little. I felt betrayed and forgotten by those who should have had my interest at heart, and I wept on.

Fiona stirred, stretched and shivered in the bedroom's clammy stuffiness. She heard my snuffling into the pillow, whipped around and lifted the blanket cautiously off my shoulders.

'What's the matter, Helen? Have you got a tummy-ache?'

Slowly, I turned my face towards her. She looked quaint with her hair neatly rolled up on hairpins secured under a net – Europe might be in flames, but Fiona set her hair every night without fail. The deep, violet blue eyes looked down at me with alarm.

'I don't really know exactly what is the matter, Fi. My tummy's all right. I just can't stop crying.'

She rolled close to me and put an arm round me. 'It must be something.'

I curled up close to her and cried into her shoulder, while she made soothing noises and stroked my long straggling locks.

Between sobs, I began to tell her about not having a student to teach and my resultant penury. She was a good listener and by no means as stupid as she sometimes led our parents to imagine. 'This last few days I've realised, Fi, that without an education – with no degree – I'll never be able to be a real social worker. I might do the same work, but I would not be as well paid. And night school doesn't provide degrees.'

Fiona smiled. 'You're clever – and you can write shorthand and type. You could get a really good secretarial job.'

'Not the way I look,' I lamented. 'My clothes are all right nowadays for social work – one shouldn't look too smart. But a secretary must look really nice.'

'You should ask Mummy. She'd buy you some clothes – she's got plenty of money – she buys all mine.'

I felt the hysteria returning. I burst into further muffled wails. 'Mother expects me to manage.' I did not want to remind her that both she and Mother preyed on me for the bits of clothing I managed to obtain for myself.

Fiona pushed my hair back from my face and said earnestly, 'I didn't think you were interested in clothes and things like that. You're always too busy.'

'Nobody thinks.' I shot at her bitterly. 'I just don't really exist where most people are concerned.'

She stared at me uncomprehendingly, as the tears came down on her nightgown in rivulets.

She hugged me tightly. 'Please, please, don't cry, Helen. If clothes are the trouble, it's easy enough for Mother to get them.'

'It's not only that,' I wept. 'I want to have fun and go dancing, like the detective said.'

This made Fiona lean back and look at me in astonishment. 'Really?'

'Well, of course I do,' I nearly bawled.

'I thought you liked studying – and books – and helping people.'

I gave up, and cried on, and a bewildered Fiona held me tightly, until her nightgown was thoroughly wet.

Downstairs Father's footsteps echoed in the hall and a moment later the front door slammed. The key hanging from the letter box by its piece of string made a protesting rattle against the wooden panels. Father, I guessed, was going for his usual Sunday morning walk and drink at Peter's, a famous public house near Catherine Street.

Mother's slippers flip-flapped up the stairs and I clung closer to Fiona. Over me crawled my infantile fear of Mother, primitive, childlike, ridiculous, but nevertheless overwhelming.

'How are you feeling?' she inquired to the back of my head buried in Fiona's shoulder. 'Crying again? Come on, that won't do. There's no need to weep so much.' The voice was kind, a little weary.

Fiona, bigger and stronger than me, pushed me away from her and eased me round to face Mother.

I made an effort to check the waterfall, and sniffed and said, 'I'm sorry, Mummy.'

Fiona burst in. 'Mummy, she's feeling miserable. But all she really needs is to look nice to get another job – and have some boy friends – and things.' She spoke cheerily and patted me. 'Isn't it, Helen? That's all.'

In part she was right, so I nodded. How could I explain my frantic need to feel that someone cared, that another adult loved me enough to really care what happened to me.

Mother had not yet washed, and she looked as badly as ever I did, with her dyed black hair in a ruffled mop and the lines on her pasty-white face looking as if they had been etched in. But she laughed, an unusually natural laugh, and sat down with a bounce on the bed. She spoke with determined cheerfulness.

'Your Father and I have been discussing the matter,' she announced.

I tried to stop crying and to listen. I did not know that I had frightened them both very much by my sudden collapse, which they feared was the beginning of a complete breakdown, with all its future slurs on the mental stability of the family. In those days one was, to most of the population, either sane or insane – and insanity marked the whole family, not just the victim.

'We think that you and Fiona must be treated alike.' I felt Fiona stiffen beside me – and suddenly I wanted to laugh, in spite of her sympathy. Did she fear being reduced to my circumstances? Mother continued, 'Daddy and I can manage if you pay into the house the same amount as Fiona does – and we'll get you some clothes out of pawn.'

I gazed at her dully. I wanted her to take me in her arms. I didn't care about the physical help. I was mentally begging her to love me, to tell me that she would do what she could to help me, sympathise, comfort.

She was waiting for my reaction, and shrugged her cardigan up closer round her neck. She became un-comfortable under my gaze and said suddenly and defensively, 'You were always so keen on managing alone.'

I was astonished, and I stopped crying. How could she rationalise the situation like that? But there was no strength in me. After all, hadn't I wanted to be treated like Fiona? And, as far as physical needs were concerned, that was what she was offering.

I had no stamina left. One cannot argue a person into loving one, so I ignored her last remark and said, 'Thank you. It would help a lot if I paid like Fiona – and I would be grateful for some clothes.' I leaned against Fiona and tried by closing my eyes tight to stop a further flood.

There was silence for a moment, while Fiona hugged me close, and then Mother said, 'Your hair is a mess. Lady Fayre is having a sale of perms. They're down to three and sixpence. I'll stand you one, if you like.'

Fiona burst in enthusiastically. 'You should, Helen. You should. Betty is a wizard on hair.'

I crushed down the pain within, and said, 'That's very kind of you, Mummy. I would love to have my hair done professionally.'

Mother really was trying to be supportive; I realised it, and I added, 'Thanks, Mum,' while I clung to the comforting warmth of Fiona, and I lay quietly while the two of them swiftly planned my physical rebuilding.

Chapter twenty-four

I sat bolt upright in the hairdresser's shabby, white, wooden chair, while Betty, a plump and gloriously brassy blonde, first removed the too small, black-rimmed glasses and then pulled out the hairpins which held my bun in place. She ran her fingers through the tumbling locks and spread them on my shoulders.

'Goodness, you've got lovely hair, Miss. So thick. I'll put a brightener in the rinse.'

I had given Betty *carte blanche* as to how she did my hair, so I smiled and said, 'Thank you.'

She took her scissors out of her pink overall pocket and snipped and shaped. Rolls of nut-brown hair joined the piles from earlier customers, drifting about the floor. She leaned me over a grey sink, which smelled of old soap and hair, and scrubbed my head with light experienced fingers, and then towelled it half-dry. Strand after strand was rolled on metal curlers, which hung round my head like so many small, clock pendulums. Cotton wool was then poked between them to protect the skull. I gasped as the curlers were doused with a chemical that smelled like ammonia, and I snatched the towel from the sink edge, to protect my smarting eyes.

Betty laughed, and threaded the curlers into plugs dangling from electric wires attached to a kind of chandelier hanging from the ceiling. She turned on a wall switch and after a second or two a strong smell of burning hair was added to that of the ammonia-like lotion. I peeped over the towel. Wisps of smoke were rising from the curlers. 'Good heavens!' I exclaimed in alarm, and instinctively tried to jerk my head away, but I was firmly suspended from the ceiling.

'Be careful,' warned Betty, 'or you'll bring the whole thing down on your head.'

Quite undisturbed by the smoke, Betty had seized a broom and was shoving the mass of cut hair into a corner, while she sang under her breath. I froze in my seat and was relieved to find that the curlers ceased to smoke.

I began to relax, and Betty went to gossip with her apprentice, who was setting another customer's hair. The apprentice looked most fashionable to my untutored eyes. She wore her hair parted down the left side, smoothed back from her face and caught in a hair slide. A loose wave nearly covered her right eye. At the shoulder the hair was turned under in what was called a page-boy. Her eyebrows had been plucked to a pencil-thin line, the expressionless face powdered to a smooth whiteness and the lips painted with a purplish lipstick to a full pout. I sighed.

My mind was dull and lethargic, sodden with weeping, which from time to time tended to burst forth without warning. I felt I never wanted to face another whining client, no matter how pitiable her state, never open another book to study, never do an iota more of housekeeping or child-caring, never ever have to face another fight.

But life does not stand still. It has to be faced, somehow dealt with. I was shamefacedly silent before the family.

On the Monday evening after my collapse, Mother had announced that she was going to the pawnbroker, and had enrolled a protesting Fiona to act as parcel carrier. 'Somebody I know might see me,' she wailed ineffectually. Now a pile of crumpled garments awaited washing and ironing or sponging and pressing, to get the smell of the pawnbroker's loft out of them. I was grateful but still leadenly depressed.

That same evening, Father had gently suggested that we might go for a walk together, and I had thankfully accepted. Numbly, I had walked beside him down the hill towards the town. We strolled along Bold Street, looking in the shop windows. It was still light enough to see their contents. Because of the blackout, no illumination had been turned on, and, since rationing had not yet begun, the windows were still filled with goods. It did not seem to have occurred to shopowners that, if we were bombed, the glass would be blown out and their careful displays ruined or looted. Wholesale looting by fellow townsmen was as yet an unbelievable idea.

Father began to play his favourite game of If I Had a Million I Would . . . With this million, he would build and furnish a huge house. I slowly began to join in. We chose furniture and curtains and rugs out of Waring and Gillows'. We filled the larder with peaches in brandy and caviare from Cooper's in

Church Street, and the butler's pantry with silver knives and forks and serving dishes from Russell's. Russell's clock struck as we walked, its little figures coming out and performing as the strokes went on, and I felt a poignant need for Baby Edward, who loved this clock, and was now trying to be a model small boy for his aunts.

We went up Lord Street and filled our imaginary wardrobes with clothes from Frisby Dykes and the many gentlemen's shops; passed the statue of Queen Victoria standing firmly above Liverpool's most popular public lavatory, and down James Street. Here we were amongst the offices of the great shipping and food companies which had their business in Liverpool. Each door had a pile of sandbags round the entrance.

The city was very quiet, as we continued on. Its peace and the pleasant conversation, my Father walking by me as he had done when I was a child, had its effect. I began to feel more cheerful.

'Let's go right down to the Pier Head,' I suggested, quite unaware that this small decision was to make a big change in my life.

The sharp wind, clean and bracing, blew up from the river, sending little eddies of abandoned wrapping papers scurrying across the sets of Mann Island.

Father held his trilby firmly on his head and I took my hat off, as the playful breeze struck us while we walked along Georges landing stage and watched the busy river glinting in the sunshine. A transatlantic liner was moored by the Princes landing stage, and, by common consent, we went to peep at it through the open gates. A good-humoured guard warned us that we must not go through the gateway, unless we had business with the ship. I looked with awe at the great Cunarder, a queen of the Atlantic.

'Nice old girl, isn't she?' remarked the guard, nodding his grey head towards the ship. He laughed ruefully, 'Not that I'd recommend a trip on her at present. It's much too lively out there for comfort.'

My hairpins were falling out in the wind, and I held on to my loosened bun while I smiled at the guard and nodded, though the thought of the German submarines lurking in Liverpool Bay was no laughing matter. Some men standing near looked as if they might be crew from the ship; they were laughing and talking as if they did not have a care in the world.

Suddenly, as Father chatted with the guard, my hair rolled down my back and was lifted up by a particularly strong gust of wind. I snatched at it and knocked off my glasses. The same gust blew up my skirts, and to the amusement of the men talking, I tried to grab at the falling glasses, the flying hair and the revealing skirts.

One man, standing with feet giving to the rise and fall of the floating dock as if used to it, laughed at me and came forward and rescued my glasses, fortunately unbroken. He was a burly young man, heavy shouldered, and with a big fair moustache, unusual for those days. As he handed me the spectacles, he looked so jolly that, unhesitatingly, I laughed back when the errant wind flicked the ash off his cigarette on to his suit. Struggling with my flying locks, I thanked him, and with Father turned towards the protection of a shed on Georges Stage. I screwed up my bun again, and we took the tram home.

It was a happy walk and I suddenly felt much better. I forgot the young man. But he did not forget me.

Betty undid a roller and tush-tushed over it, rolled it up and slipped it back into its electric outlet. 'Won't be long now,' she remarked, as she leaned against the sink and lit a cigarette. Through the cigarette smoke, she looked me over in a casual, friendly way. 'Yer sister says you never go anywhere. But, yer know, yer could do quite well for yourself – if yer wanted.' She turned to her assistant who was standing turning the pages of a magazine, while she waited for her customer's hair to dry under a noisy machine. 'Couldn't she, Dawn?'

Dawn flicked her cigarette ash into the sink and strolled over to look me over, as if I was a pony up for sale. She nodded, and smiled at me. 'You got lovely legs.'

'Wait till I've finished her hair. You won't know her,' promised Betty. 'If you like, luv, I'll make your face up, too. Just so you can see what a difference it can make.'

'O.K.'

Underneath still surged a fearful depression hard to control, despite Mother and Father being so helpful, an emptiness of spirit, a lack of hope.

I was unable to talk truthfully and naturally to my parents, was certain in my mind that as soon as I seemed better, their interest would wane again. I missed the children and the letters from Friedrich and Ursel, all of whom had at least diverted my mind from our grim surroundings. I had not seen Sylvia for some days and determined that some of my new pocket money would be spent in order to see more of her. But even with her, there was a holding back, a reserve, a sense that I would never make her understand what the years had done to me. That trust was to come later on, but its time had not yet arrived.

I was thrust under a spray and Betty's scarlet tipped fingers scrubbed away the ghastly smelling solution. In apprehension I watched her brush out the tiny tight curls until I looked like a South Sea Islander. 'Goodness, Betty. What are you doing?'

Betty laughed, and sloshed highly scented setting lotion over my head. Cold trickles ran down my neck. 'Haven't you ever had a perm before, luv?'

'No,' I admitted shyly. 'I've not been to a hairdresser before.'

'Well, I never. You wait. Proper pretty it will be.'

And proper pretty it was. Soft curls finally haloed my thin face, a deep wave disguising the high forehead.

Betty stepped back and looked at me, head on one side. 'Now, when it grows, I'll set it for you with a bush of curls at the back – you could put a big slide in to hold them. T' perm'll last a few months, if you vary the style a bit.' She leaned over me, and picked up a pair of tweezers from the shelf in front of us. 'Now hold still.' She put a heavy hand on my forehead, and gave a quick series of painful tweaks with her tweezers. 'See, I took a few hairs out between your brows – makes a difference, doesn't it?' It did.

She took her own make-up from out of her hand-bag and swiftly rubbed vanishing cream into my face, touched the cheeks very lightly with rouge, carefully crayoned the lips with a slightly mauve lipstick, added a little length to the heavy black eyebrows with a dark pencil, and stood back. 'Come and see, Dawn. What she needs is very soft make-up, looking so young, like.'

Dawn, her customer combed out and sent on her way, strolled languidly over. 'Very nice,' she opined. 'Boy friends won't know you.'

I blushed under the rouge. 'I don't go in for boy friends.' Then at their startled looks, I added, 'Never had time.'

'For crying out loud!' Betty exclaimed. 'You've missed your vocation – you could do real well for yourself. You look as nice as the next girl – and you walk a lot nicer. Why Nick was only saying the other day, you got style – only needs bringing out.'

Astonished, I asked, 'Who's Nick?'

'Oh, you know him. Everybody does. He knows you. He was in this morning, fiddling with everything as usual. Saw your name in the Appointments Book. He knows every girl in the place – it's his business.' She giggled.

'But I don't know him,' I insisted, preparing to get up from the chair.

'Oh, yeah, yer must do. He's often around the Rialto – wears a light coloured mac most of the time – proper smart.'

Enlightment dawned. 'Oh, yes. He says good night

sometimes.' I paused, and looked at her distrustfully. 'But he's a pimp.'

The girls grinned knowingly at each other. 'Sure. He's set up a lot of girls in his time. Buys 'em clothes. Finds them flats. He's fair. Trades under a lamp-post, he does. Yer should get to know him better – you'd do fine with him. He moves his best girls into real good districts.'

I was shocked. 'Oh, Betty. I'm not that kind.'

Betty's face lost its smile, and hardened. 'We're all that kind, luv, when times are like they are. Better'n slaving in service or standing on your feet in a factory all day – or being so clemmed like you are.'

I looked at her steadily. There were lines under the heavy make-up. I got slowly up from the chair. Did she find it better than being a hairdresser who had to cut prices to the bone? 'Thank you, Betty,' I said very gently, and I took out from my otherwise empty handbag the three and sixpence which Mother had given me, and handed it to her, while Dawn drifted back to her magazines.

Betty smiled very sweetly at me, as she put the money into the drawer of a chipped, white counter. She replied a little sadly. 'There, luv. Don't be offended. You take care of yourself – and keep that innocent face of yours. Some nice lad'll know a good thing when he sees it – and take proper care of you.'

'You're too flattering, Betty,' I teased her. 'I'm not cross.' She meant to be kind and I did not want to leave her with the feeling that I condemned her way of life. I knew from my work that, too often, it carried with it its own tragic punishments.

Chapter twenty-five

I went back to work on the Tuesday after my collapse, and did my best to cope with the mob besieging our waiting room. It was a week later, however, when I walked into the office with hair permed, face made up, dressed in a good blue tweed suit and a plain white blouse, and caused a modest sensation.

'My goodness,' exclaimed my patient colleague, her pale face turned upwards from a mass of untidy files lying on her desk. 'I can see you won't be with us long, if you go on looking like that,' she added archly. 'You look very pretty.'

The inference that I might be whisked off to the altar at any moment made me smile weakly, as I teetered on my second-hand high-heeled shoes towards the door, and hung one of Mother's old hats on the back of it. The hat was navy blue and Fiona had donated a bunch of artificial sweet peas to retrim it. Both Mother and Fiona had been unexpectedly kind in helping to renovate a crushed young woman. But the inner woman remained squashed.

It would be nice to be able to say that we lived in amity ever after. Far from it. Mother continued to nag at Father and rage at me, between short bouts of better humour. Father still drank more than he could afford, still lost his temper over small details. Mother and Fiona, rushing to get ready for work, still purloined any clean clothes I had. But the total of garments between us was greater.

The amount of expense money and pocket money seemed wonderful. It bought a meagre lunch, stockings, and make-up from Woolworth's. I bought some much needed panties and a petticoat, all as yet unrationed. I was close to having the comforts of the working-class girls who sat facing me on the long benches of the trams, as I went to work. I was servilely grateful to my parents.

I was so afraid of offending people, particularly Father and Mother, that I was finding it increasingly difficult to show any originality, to use my own judgment. For years, I had continued a deadly routine of night school, of being an exact and obedient employee, an inoffensive helper at home – except when human nature had its say and I burst into a temper.

Now at aged twenty I wanted to strike out, find a new life for myself. To learn to act, not just react. I had been brain-washed too long into the idea that I lived by courtesy of other people. Touched as yet lightly by the first ripples of tremendous social change which was to affect all women, I determined to change myself not only in appearance but in character, to assert myself, to be a whole woman in my own right.

'I am me,' I cried inside. 'And I want to be me.'

Mother agreed to Sylvia's coming to tea. I wanted to learn from this most faithful friend's outlook on life. She was so balanced, so sensible.

Sylvia came. Her hair was, as usual, carefully blonded, swept upwards from the back to form a crown of curls on top of her head. The fairness complimented speedwell blue eyes and a dimpled, merry face. She talked with Mother and made her laugh. They got on splendidly.

Sylvia had always taken a course or two at night school, and because all schools were closed she was wondering, like me, what to do with her spare time. Now, as she sat like a neutral zone between Mother and me, I made a great effort to advance an idea made possible by the advent of some pocket money.

'You know, Sylvia, how clumsy I am – I'm always dropping things or falling over something. And I was wondering if I learned to dance – that would help me. After all, you learn to be precise in your movements when you dance.' I paused doubtfully. I did not dare to say in front of Mother that the detective had left with me this idea of dancing, having fun. I feared her scornful laughter, in spite of her recent efforts on my behalf. 'I wondered if we could go together?'

Sylvia drew in a deep breath. She was a nonconformist by religious persuasion, and with a sinking heart I remembered suddenly that nonconformists do not dance. Perhaps I've shocked her, I thought miserably.

Fiona interjected, 'I never had to *learn* to dance – I just picked it up.'

I ignored Fiona. I hoped that dancing was all her devoted retinue had tried to teach her, but in my jealous heart I always knew that, though Fiona seemed so pliable, her escorts would not be allowed to step out of line. She had a firm fastidiousness bordering on the prudish – she enjoyed the turmoil she created, but she would laugh and slip away from any man who presumed too far.

I concentrated on Sylvia. She was happily ladling jam on to a thin wafer of bread and butter. A quarter of a pound of butter had been bought specially for her, and the bread had been cut as it used to be cut in our long ago world of cooks and housemaids.

'Everything is shut,' she said ruefully.

'There are two or three dance studios tucked into old houses round here,' I reminded her. 'One of them says on its noticeboard that it charges only a shilling for a group lesson.' What was Sylvia thinking? Was she feeling wicked at the idea of dancing?

'I used to go to ballet school when I was little,' I went on, 'until a wardrobe fell on top of me and injured my foot – and it was great fun. After that I dragged the foot a bit, but I should be all right for ballroom dancing.' I could not mention that such a corrupt person as Nick said that I walked well – and had style.

She made a little moue with her mouth. 'That must have hurt. Of course, I'll come if you would like to go.' She giggled as if she thought it might be fun.

'You can dance already,' Mother protested. 'Why waste money? We sent you to learn ballroom dancing, when you made such a fuss about not going to ballet school any more.' She looked at me accusingly, as if I should now emerge, twelve years later, a perfect dancer – like a moth crawling out of a chrysalis and taking flight.

I did not say anything. I sensed the beginning of a fight which I had not the strength to undertake.

'Oh, she'll have forgotten,' Sylvia assured Mother briskly, as if she understood my need to be rescued before I fled back down my mental burrow. She turned to me, and added firmly, 'See what day they take beginners, and give me a phone call at the office. I'll come.'

Chapter twenty-six

The black taffeta dress with tiny gold spots on it was redeemed from pawn and carefully pressed. I had made it several years before from a length of material bought from the pawnbroker. It had been cut out with a razor blade and hand stitched. The taffeta smelled old, but the dress had not split anywhere. New black lace frilling was sewn into its neckline. Also redeemed were the white satin slippers I had worn at my Confirmation. I dyed them black. They had satin bows on each toe, and I was entranced by them; they looked so delightfully frivolous. Cinderella was about to go to the ball.

Cinderella, however, was not actively expecting to meet a prince. At the back of her mind lay the memory of the pleasure of moving rhythmically to music, a faint picture of a small girl in a short black velvet tunic standing in front of a mirror and slowly rising on her first pair of points, a child dreaming of being a cygnet in *Swan Lake*.

The cygnet was still rather like a duck, as she climbed the stone front steps to the porticoed entrance of the dancing school. The paint was peeling off the front door, and the steps looked as if they had not been swept for a generation.

Emboldened by a tiny crack of light from under the

door and the distant sound of a gramophone, Sylvia rang the bell.

The door was opened by a thin man in a light grey business suit. Hair was plastered back from a middle parting, above a rather sickly face. Grey eyes, as sharp as the Warden's when looking for illicit cracks of light, surveyed the two of us.

We both smiled politely, while the unfriendly stare continued. Then suddenly the man grinned. 'Come in, come in,' he invited, and led us into a big, dimly lit hall from which a wide staircase led upwards into total darkness. He closed the door quickly behind us, and inquired, 'Are you beginners?'

We assured him that we both had to start from scratch. 'Well,' he exclaimed jovially, rubbing his hands, 'Tonight's the night. We'll soon have you on your feet.' He pointed to a cupboard under the staircase. 'Put your coats in there. Bring your handbags with you – we mustn't lose things, must we? Then you can give Doris here your shilling.'

As we took off our coats, I observed a smiling middle-aged woman in a frilly dress covered with a pattern of large orange flowers. She held a record in her hand, and put it down on a small hall table, while we paid her.

'Ever been dancin' before?' she inquired in a friendly voice.

'No,' we murmured bashfully.

'Oh, you'll enjoy yourselves here. You'll like the people. We're fussy who we have in. No trouble – ever.'

Trouble in connection with a dancing school had not occurred to me, and I wondered timorously what she meant, but the man came bustling in from the hall saying, 'I'm Norm,' and led us further into the ballroom.

The ballroom had been contrived by the removal of the walls between the dining room, sitting room and breakfast room in the original house, so that the dance floor ran from front to back of the building. Three sets of windows were heavily shrouded with blackout curtains. The walls were a faded, frowsy grey, and battered bentwood chairs lined two sides. A large glass-fronted cabinet stood in an alcove at one end. On a small table, by the door through which we had entered, stood a big wind-up gramophone, flanked by an untidy stack of records. Two girls in summery dresses sat, legs crossed, on the far side of the room. Cigarettes dangled from their fingers, and they glanced casually over at us, and then continued their animated conversation. A couple of young men in neat suits with wide flowing trouser legs and big, gaudily striped ties were sprinkling chalk on the hardwood floor which, alone, showed evidence of care. The surface had been lovingly refinished and the wood glowed.

Norm seated us near the other girls, and said, 'I'll be back,' as the doorbell rang. Doris put on a record, and the young men rubbed the chalk lightly with their feet along the line of dance.

Men and women in their twenties and three or four much older couples began to fill up the room. Most of them seemed to know each other, and, while they waited, they gossiped in thick nasal Liverpool accents. Doris changed the record to a quick-step, winding up the gramophone like a mangle. She and Norm then swept out on to the floor and danced, while everybody watched. Since this was only the second time I had seen adults dancing, I was no judge, but the couple made a production of a basically simple dance. An infinite number of graceful variations was introduced, and, oblivious of their audience, they smiled at each other as if sharing some rapturous experience. It was a wonderful exhibition of perfectly coordinated, flowing movement; the shabby room was for a few minutes a theatre. I did not know then that I was looking at two of the best ballroom dancers in the north.

With hands clenched tightly on my lap, knees and ankles primly together, I sat on the edge of my chair, mesmerised by the charm of the dance. Now Doris and Norm gave a little bow, the audience clapped, and they retreated towards the gramophone. After a moment of consultation with his partner, Norm strode into the middle of the room, rubbed his hands together, and said, 'Now, most of yez learned the basic steps of the waltz last week. Now I want you to try out what you learned, and then we'll learn how to do a turn. Take your partners, please.'

The two girls smoking near us screwed their cigarette ends into a saucer of nub ends on the floor by their chairs, and rose to partner each other. I flashed a tiny, scared smile at Sylvia, who was sitting leaning back in her chair with a bright smile on her face. A young man, immaculately neat, acne scars all over his face, crossed the floor to her, and, with work-roughened hands clasped before him, bowed and asked her, 'Would you like to dance?'

She blushed, pushed her handbag surreptitiously further under her chair with her toe, and with a cheery grin at me, announced, 'Well – er, I can't dance.'

The young man went pink, and replied that he could not either. Undaunted, they went out on to the floor, and the young man put his arm round her waist, clasping her as if she might run away at any moment.

I was alone, feeling a little rejected. Would nobody ask me?

Norm was checking his flock, and when he found everybody paired off except me, he bowed and said, 'Let's dance, love.'

I remembered how to stand, and put my hand correctly on to his shoulder. He smelled nicely of carbolic soap and brilliantine. 'Now, everybody,' he called, 'remember, one and two, one and two, one and two.'

A very firm hand at my waist and an equally firm grasp of my right hand led me off correctly, without a word being said, except for the chanting count of 'one and two'. We circled the floor. After the first few steps the beat of the big band music relaxed me and I allowed myself to flow with my partner. 'Good,' he murmured approvingly, and twirled me into a simple variation. 'Very good.'

'You can dance already,' he said puzzled, 'and you're very light.'

I blushed to the roots of my hair, as if I had done something wrong. 'Well, I learned as a very little girl, but I thought I'd forgotten,' I confessed. Then I got up enough courage to say shyly, 'I think that it is your good guidance. I've never seen anybody dance like you and Doris. I wish I could be that good.'

He seemed as pleased with the compliment as if I had presented him with yet another gold cup, to add to the collection in the cabinet. Then he said, 'Oh, aye. You might be if you stuck at it.' He added earnestly, 'You'd have to find yourself a good partner, though. We've got a few silver medallists as come here – working for their golds, they are – and we've got one gold medallist – other than ourselves, that is.'

As the record came to an end, he led me over to Doris. 'We'll try the turn now,' he said to her. Then he added, 'Been telling this young lady, what's your name, luv, that she could win a silver if she worked.'

Doris nodded. 'I was watching you.'

I said shyly, 'My name is Helen Forrester. I didn't know one could get medals for dancing.'

'Of course you can,' replied Doris. 'A silver means you're good – and a gold you can teach.'

I looked at her open-mouthed. She had just bounced right at my feet a most interesting, brand new idea of how I might earn a living. Long ago, a country doctor had broken it to me very gently that I could never be a ballet dancer, because I was going to walk always with one foot turned slightly in. My dancing teacher confirmed it. I was sent to learn ball-room dancing, because every middle-class girl was expected to be able to dance. I had been very un-happy amid hordes of other little girls, and small boys dressed in sailor suits with whistles hung round their necks or in Eton suits with stiff white collars. Nobody had seemed to notice the turned foot – and neither, apparently, had Norm or Doris.

Doris was saying proudly, 'You should look at our cups in the cabinet there – proper collection of 'em we've got. Going to try for the world championship soon.'

None of us seemed to think it strange to talk about entering dance competitions, when we expected to be bombed out of existence before too long.

'How exciting!' I exclaimed, with genuine enthusiasm.

'Needs a lot of work,' Norm said, as he sifted through the worn records. He picked out a record and handed it to Doris to put on to the gramophone. While she was doing this, he leaned against the table to rest his feet, and said to me, 'If you're serious, you should come for lessons at least twice a week, and then come to the dance on Saturday night for practice with different partners. See how you get on, like.' He smiled at me, and I agreed, and then said shyly, 'I think I'd better go back to Sylvia.'

Sylvia was making rueful remarks about broken toes to the girl next to her. I sat down primly on the edge of the chair beside her. I was determined to continue the classes, and I hoped she would come with me, so I said soothingly, 'Never mind. A few lessons and we'll all improve.'

My dance with Norm had not gone unnoticed, and the moment we were told to take our partners to learn the turn, a gawky young man with a nervously bobbing Adam's apple was at my elbow, bowing with old-fashioned politeness to ask me if I cared to dance.

224

I jumped up eagerly, like an unpopular child suddenly asked to join in a game.

Norm, I discovered, was a stickler for good ballroom manners, and he stormed down the room towards one youth who asked a girl in a pink blouse, 'Worm, come and wiggle.'

'If that's how you're going to address a nice young lady, you needn't bother to come again,' he snapped.

The nice young lady immediately sat up straight, folded her hands in her lap and lowered her eyes.

The boy made a wry face, swept her a low bow, and inquired, 'Madam, would you care to dance?'

She nodded assent and rose gravely, leaving her cigarette balanced on an ash tray. Satisfied, Norm turned to his class.

Sylvia's pretty face and cheery manner assured her of partners, and I sat out only one dance. From this predicament I was rescued by Doris, who took the man's part and guided me very well through the basic steps of the slow foxtrot, which I had not danced before.

As we groped our way carefully through the unlit streets, towards the stop where Sylvia could catch a tram home, I was animated, flushed with excitement and exercise, yet scared that for some reason I might not be able to afford to go to the class again.

Sylvia's face was scarcely visible, but from the tone of her remarks she seemed to view the evening with an easy good humour and would tolerate another evening like it. My spirits sank a little, and I wondered if she could possibly understand what a lifeline it seemed to me.

Chapter twenty-seven

After a couple of weeks, Sylvia gave up attending the dancing classes, because of the long distance she had to travel in the blackout.

I went on my own. All the girls there were very nice to me, though they never gossiped with me or shared their jokes. Norm and Doris were conscientious teachers; and I began to gain a little self-confidence.

The dancing of the silver medallists at the Saturday evening dance showed a finish which owed much to almost daily practice. I was astonished at how much time working-class people were willing to spend on it, unlike the upper classes, who had many other sources of entertainment. Amongst Norm's pupils were older married couples who had met at a dance club, and had danced together all their adult lives.

To dance had been my first ambition in life and the first to be crushed. Its relaxing rhythm now began to heal the wounds that earlier years in Liverpool had so painfully inflicted upon me.

If I wanted to continue to dance, I had also to learn to be courteous and sociable. Such skills are normally learned within the family and their circle, while playing games, attending parties or church or clubs. By extreme poverty and the need to be a surrogate mother, I had been cut off from all the contacts that a young girl could normally expect to enjoy. Now, at twenty, I was an ignorant novice, trying to pick her way amid people who would have roared with laughter at most of the ideas with which my brain was cluttered. It was not easy.

The young men must have had many quiet laughs at my clumsy efforts to be agreeable. I was painfully shy with them, and soon became aware that they treated me a little differently from the other girls present. It was subtle, but it was there. I was an oddity.

I never lacked partners, because I swam on to the dance floor with the ease of a baby duckling learning to swim. All of them wanted a good partner with whom to practise, regardless of whom they eventually escorted home after the dance.

One brave youngster, curly haired and with the physique of a boxer, did one Saturday evening ask if he could take me home. I looked at him with short-sighted bewilderment and assured him that I was quite capable of seeing myself home. He looked stunned for a moment – perhaps he had never been refused before – and then he grinned in a friendly way which seemed to indicate approval, and said, 'That's O.K., luv,' and went to ask somebody else. Word of this rebuff must have gone round the class, because nobody else ventured to ask.

I went to the classes as frequently as I could afford. At first I was too shy to go to the Saturday night social dances, feeling that my dress was too shabby for a formal dance. The other girls seemed to have innumerable dresses.

I was so accustomed to working as a social worker amid a sea of unemployed, that I had never realised that even if unemployment was 33%, that still left over 66% of people in employment.

Now I was entering a new world of highly skilled artisans, where the division of the sexes was amply demonstrated by the fact that the women, whether married or not, congregated on one side of the room, while the men stood on the other side. Occasionally, bored by the lack of conversation, I would talk with Norm and Doris and learned much about their dancing careers and their hopes of expanding their business when the war was over – maybe after next Christmas.

I discovered that I was supposed to talk to my partners while dancing, and I spent anxious moments trying to think of something to amuse men whose main interests were football, football pools, girls and learning to dance so that one could meet more girls.

Finally, I hit on the question, 'Do you work round here?' This usually got an immediate answer, and then I would ask what their job was. This usually called forth a monologue which lasted until the dance ended. As I was escorted back to my chair, I would assure them that it had been a really interesting conversation and I had no idea before how hard men worked. It was true. Many of them worked very hard in hot, dirty, dangerous places, and I soon admired their tenacity, and the fact that they never seemed to realise how brave they were. One of them had spent most of his working life setting the stones of the Anglican Cathedral, and was very angry at having been brought down to street level by a government call-up, to build air raid shelters.

I met mechanics and carpenters, electricians and apprentice plumbers, machinists, pattern makers, draughtsmen, shipyard workers, slaughtermen, engineers of every description, bakers and others who worked in Liverpool's huge food industry, occasionally a man in an ill-fitting uniform home on his first leave; very rarely, a seaman or two. They were all scrubbed from head to heel, hair clipped close to their heads like Roman soldiers, dressed in well-pressed Sunday suits.

The top earners were girls who worked for Vernon's and Littlewood's, the companies who ran the football pools. Other girls were shop assistants, waitresses, factory hands in the biscuit factories or stocking works or the Dunlop Rubber Company. They dressed most elaborately, and I gathered from overheard conversations that they spent hours shopping for exactly matching hats, gloves and shoes, and in setting each other's hair. Like the girls I had worked with in the head office of my employers, they talked only of men, films and clothes.

On Sundays, I often went for a walk with Father. He gave me not only time but long and stimulating discussions of subjects which interested him. There was little that he had not studied of the life and times of Louis XIV of France, le Roi Soleil. We would discuss the King's policies, his strengths and failings, the details of his palace of Versailles, which Father had visited a number of times in his youth, and the lives of his advisers.

At night, we turned on our rickety radio, and Mother, Father and I listened to the nine o'clock news, as if it were holy writ. Then we would sweep the seeking needle slowly across the dial, while we tried to pick up news from France and Germany; and more than once I heard Hitler making a speech which sounded all the more terrifying because I could not always understand all of it.

Both Father and Mother benefited from a quieter home. Father never said whether he missed the younger members of his family and he never went to see them, probably because he flinched at the thought of having to meet his sisters if he did.

So, while Poland fought for its very existence, I danced my way back to a modicum of mental health, and we all waited for the holocaust to begin. The thought of it sat at the back of everybody's mind, a weight only hinted at by some stray remark – but there, all the same. At that time in the war, it was as if a conductor had raised his baton ready to begin a symphony, and the tiny pause before the orchestra played the first chord went on and on and on, the players frozen in their seats.

Chapter twenty-eight

People who did not drink were thankful to find some entertainment still open to them, and Norm was having to turn people away. 'T' floor might collapse and land us all in t' cellar, if I get too many dancing at the same time,' he explained, his thin face earnest. His skin looked yellow from too many late nights, on top of a job in a grocery during the day.

To me, the vibrations of the floor suddenly became something in which to take a personal interest.

Normally the Saturday night dance brought out the best dancers, Norm's treasured silvers and gold, and they now became fretful at the overcrowding. He consoled them by quietly opening up on Sunday night for them. Fortunately for him, the police had plenty of other work on their hands.

I still occasionally went to church on Sunday evenings, though the religious ardour of my early teens had gone. There was still enough natural light for the services to take place. The days of services in semi-darkness, as the winter approached, were yet to come. I would sit in the back pew, as usual, and wonder how I should make a life for myself, and sometimes ask divine help. Ever since I had arrived in Lime Street station at the age of eleven, torn from all that was familiar to me, I had seen clearly the need to obtain an education, despite my parents' objections, and then find an occupation to make me financially independent. What else could a plain girl look forward to? Now the war had made life even more complicated. Though I had not been able to find other employment, there was a steady flow of women, bereft of their menfolk, leaving their homes to take men's places in the work force. There was a call for volunteers for the women's services, in the Army, Navy and Air Force; but because I had no formal educational qualifications, I shrank from being thrown into the lowest rank to do unskilled, menial tasks. Less and less, I wanted to spend my whole life in the sea of sorrow in which I was at present working. I was recovered enough to feel compassion for the flood of widows caused by the sinking of the *Athenia* and the *Courageous* and a myriad of small ships which had been caught far from home at the outbreak of hostilities, and were now trying to creep back to Britain through seas menaced by U-boats. But sometimes I longed for laughter and cheerfulness. And so, while the collection clinked into the church plate, I fretted absently.

August and September saw Fiona's young escorts increasingly likely to be in uniform. It was clear that *my* dancing partners were going to be the war's privileged class; their skills were needed in the factories, much too precious to be wasted on the battlefield. It seemed that the war was going to be actually fought by the upper classes and by life's eternal losers, the unskilled.

It was Saturday, the day on which Hitler and Stalin formally abolished the country of Poland; and the clear moonlight made a fairyland of black Liverpool, beating its slate roofs into silver sheets, softening the ugly row houses, making the grubby windowpanes glitter and the eyes of the many slinking cats in the alleys into blazing emeralds, as if there could not be a war in progress. It was a night of calm in which to look at the newly rediscovered stars.

Swinging my dancing shoes on two fingers, I strolled leisurely along the avenue to the dance club. Except for the bottom step, the imposing front steps and porch were in deep shadow, but I ran up them absently with feet that had become familiar with them, and stumbled clumsily into a small group of people waiting to be let in.

'Ow!' exclaimed a male voice, as, confused and apologetic, I stepped back on to a foot.

A shaded torch flashed for a second on my face, and then was turned downward to aid the shuffling and giggling group to see.

The owner of the torch assured me, 'It's all right. I think I'll live.' I was aware of a solid rock of male figure leaning against the portico.

''lo, Helen,' one of the waiting girls who had seen my illuminated face greeted me.

'Hello, Gloria,' I replied, smiling into the darkness. 'How are you?'

She did not have time to answer, because the door was opened by a grinning Norm, apologising for being so long. 'Had to go upstairs and turn a light off,' he explained.

Seven of us, four men and three women, hurried into the dimly lit hall. Though the electric light was

233

swathed in red tissue paper to dull its rays, Norm shut the door quickly, before the ever vigilant warden could complain.

The gramophone was playing a scratched record of *Three Little Fishes and a Mother Fishie, too,* as we took off our coats and changed our shoes – woe betide anyone who stepped on Norm's precious floor in anything but dancing shoes. I always put on my little satin slippers with a feeling of pure joy.

I did not know the other people who had entered with Gloria and me, so I wandered into the ballroom with her. The dance was already in full swing and the floor was crowded. Doris looked up from her gramophone records and remarked, 'You're lucky. There isn't room for any more.' She surveyed the crowded room, and then added, 'This won't last, now the big dance halls are opening up again.'

'Why not?' I queried. 'It's a friendly place.'

She sighed. 'Well, we depend on regulars, and if they keep on transferring men around the country, like they are doing, there won't be anybody left for you to dance with, luv. Our John's got to report to some dump in Hull tomorrer. And he hasn't even got a place to stay.'

Our John was her brother, a pattern maker, so I commiserated with her, while the old house shook gently with the boom of the music and the movement of the dancers.

Gloria and I were soon claimed by men who knew us and were swept away into the mêlée of dancers. Above the music, I could hear Norm greeting some of the people who had come in with me, as if they were prodigal sons. 'Where you been all this time? What you doin' now?'

My partner deposited me, breathless, on a chair on the far side of the room from the door, where the reunion was continuing with much back slapping and laughter. My perspiring partner, the bricklayer who was really a stone mason, bowed and left me, to join the male cohorts near the door. I smiled briefly at the girl sitting next to me, but did not talk. She was with her mate, her close girl friend, and absorbed in a deep conversation about what *he* did and what *he* said last night.

I was still panting, when I thought I heard my name mentioned in the group of which Norm was the centre. I looked up quickly, just in time to see Norm hastily lower a finger pointing at me. Apparently slightly embarrassed, he turned his back to me and continued the conversation, in which Doris was also included.

The cigarette smoke made the room blue, hazing faces, dimming lights and adding a further deposit to the walls and ceiling. After a slightly longer break than usual Norm shouted, 'Take your partners for an old-fashioned waltz,' and after a doubtful start the strains of The Blue Danube filled the room.

Two young men were standing before me, both wishing to dance. One was a stranger.

'Like to dance?' asked the old acquaintance, with a surly look at the newcomer.

I was about to rise, when the stranger said shamelessly, 'Little Miss Helen promised this one to me when we came in.'

I opened my mouth to rebut this indignantly, but he had already leaned down and put his hand firmly under my elbow to help me up. Before I even had time to look at him properly, I was out on the floor, making apologetic faces to the other man over my partner's shoulder.

What the man lacked in finesse, he made up in energy. An old-fashioned waltz takes more vigour than its later counterpart and was always a test of endurance for me. Nevertheless, I was laughing breathlessly by the time the Blue Danube managed to reach the sea and come to an end. We had not spoken a word, and I had hardly glanced at my partner's face, except to note that he must be in his thirties. Lines, which would soon look like seams, etched a ruddy skin lightly, and there was little of the softness of youth. The face was vaguely familiar. The arms guiding me were extremely strong.

With a final spin, he whirled me to the narrow end of the room with its case of golden trophies. We flopped on to two rarely used chairs, and he pulled a handkerchief from his top pocket and mopped a perspiring brow. Blue eyes beneath fair, bushy brows laughed at me over the damp cotton. I was panting like a Pekinese and could not speak. The eyes were so merry, though, that I had to smile back. It was as if we suddenly shared some naughty secret.

'Well, little Miss Helen, how was that?'

'Fun,' I gasped. 'But, really you told an awful lie.'

'I spend nights dreaming of meeting her again – and she calls me a liar when I do.' He slowly tucked the crumpled hanky back into his pocket, then leaned back in his uncomfortable chair, hands lying loosely on his thighs. He looked at me, with a slight smile curving under a heavy, though neat moustache somewhat yellowed by tobacco smoke. Strong stubby fingers showed faint signs also of cigarette smoke, as did most people's.

Though subjected to a fairly intense examination, I did not feel shy – only bewildered that he claimed to have met me before. He was so relaxed, however, that he conveyed it to me, and when I had regained my breath, I said perplexedly, 'I'm sorry, but I don't remember meeting you before – yet you knew my name?'

'A girl on the steps called you by it – and, anyway, Norm sent me over to dance with you – thought you'd like me. Do you?'

I burst out laughing, embarrassed by the question. I did not know what to reply. 'Well . . . well . . .' I looked again at him, and then added bravely, 'Of course.'

He grinned, more at my confusion, I think, than at the reply.

'Did I . . .? Were you . . .? Did I tread on you on the step?'

'Yes,' he responded, with a twinkle, 'You trampled on me. I'm very hard done by tonight.'

I was sober. 'Did it hurt very much? I'm so sorry.'

'I thought I was crippled for life.'

'At least you didn't swear.'

'I save that for recalcitrant machinery – and occasionally for other things. Are you accustomed to men swearing at you?'

'No. But they do swear sometimes – under their breath. And at work I've been sworn at by angry men once or twice.'

'Have you? Where do you work?'

'Well, I'm a social worker – and sometimes men don't like the advice you give them – or the advice you give their wives – and they get very miffed.'

The smile had gone from his face, and he said, 'Well, I'm blowed. You don't look like one.'

'Like what?'

'A social worker.'

'What's wrong with them?' I asked sharply. But a quickstep burst from the ever-faithful gramophone and, without answering, he got up and held out his hand to me to dance.

He held me quite closely and guided me into one or two variations which I think he had invented himself. His suit was navy blue and I was careful not to brush my powdered face against his shoulder. After we had circled the floor in silence, he asked me in a genuinely puzzled tone, 'What's a nice girl like you doing in a place like this?'

I turned my face up to his. 'It's most respectable,' I parried.

'Aye, it is. Norm takes care of that. But you're different. You don't belong here.'

His accent was that of a north country man, but he did not have the thick nasal Liverpool accent of the other men present. I grinned wickedly, and inquired with deceptive quietness, 'And what is a nice man like you doing in a place like this?'

That made him jump. 'What? Me?' I felt the quiver of laughter in him. '*Touché*,' he replied.

We danced half way round the room before he answered. Then he said, 'I came with one of my friends and his wife. I sometimes do in winter. They're great dancers – they learned here.' He twiddled me into one of his fancy variations, and I felt the smallest sigh go through him. 'I rent a room in their house – to keep my gear in – and to sleep in when I'm in Liverpool.'

I glanced up at his face again. The mouth under the moustache was set and he looked suddenly weary. He became aware of my gaze and looked down at me, and smiled.

I was feeling tired myself, so I asked, 'Would you like to sit out the rest of the dance?'

Pure mischief glinted in the blue eyes. 'That's an idea.' He guided me round until we reached the door, and under the benign eye of Norm leaning against the gramophone table, he danced me into the empty, chilly hall, and sat me down on the carpeted stairs. They smelled of dust. He squeezed in beside me. There was just room for the two of us, and he put his arm round me, ostensibly to make more space. It was exceedingly comforting, quite the snuggest feeling I had ever experienced. And I felt quite safe. Norm was only a few feet away. It struck me that Norm had allowed this man to do something he would never tolerate in anyone else. Nobody was allowed to linger in the dark hall. Everybody was kept firmly under his paternal eye in the ballroom.

'Do you know Norm and Doris well?'

'Pretty well. Been coming here occasionally for years. Makes some company when I'm ashore, if all my friends seem to be out.'

He wriggled himself more comfortably in beside me. 'Mind if I smoke?' I assured him that I did not mind, so more wriggling ensued while he retrieved cigarettes and matches from his jacket pocket. Before flicking out the match, he held it and it lit up his face. It was not a particularly handsome visage; it was somewhat battered, though full of laughter lines. The nose looked as if it had been broken long ago. The eyes were lively and intelligent. The match, of course, lit my face as well, and I wished suddenly that I was as lovely as Fiona. I had never sat alone with a man other than my father, and never close to one except Emrys Hughes during a holiday when I was about fifteen, a charity holiday obtained for me by the Presence. And Emrys Hughes had been old enough to be my father. This man was young and I wanted to continue sitting by him; it felt very nice. He had already slipped the packet of cigarettes into his top pocket, when he said contritely, 'I forgot to ask if you'd like one. Would you?'

'No, thank you. I don't smoke.'

There was a small silence between us while he drew on his cigarette, which I broke by asking, 'Do you go to sea?'

'Yes, Miss. Engineer. Got my Master's, though. And how did you know?'

'You walk like a seaman. And what is a Master's?'

'Master's Certificate. One day – maybe – I might get a ship of my own.'

'Master of your fate?' I teased.

'And Captain of my soul.' The voice had an odd, defensive note in it. The hall was cold and I began to shiver.

His arm tightened round me, and he exclaimed, 'You're getting chilled. Come on, little lady, let's dance.'

So we danced, and I heard a great deal about the problems of being an engineer. Then he was silent as he led me round the room. I forgot that there were other men with whom I normally danced. I was content to let myself float in the arms of this most peculiar man, a man who looked as tough as an old boot, yet with a speech that was almost as civilised as my own.

I remembered suddenly that he had not told me where he had met me before, and I wondered if perhaps it was a long time ago, when I had stayed with my grandmother. He might have lived in the same village.

Chapter twenty-nine

Norm put on the record with which he always closed off the evening, a waltz called *Who's Taking You Home Tonight?*

My partner was very quiet as we slowly circled the floor. He looked down at me and asked, quite humbly, 'Can I see you home?'

I was suddenly flooded with shyness. 'It's all right,' I murmured, turning my face away. 'You don't have to bother. I'm quite safe by myself.'

My face felt flushed. I looked up at him and was subjected to a sober, searching look. He sighed, and agreed, 'You're quite right, my dear. When are you coming here again?'

'Tuesday, all being well.'

'Well, I'll see you here. It'll be a day or two yet before we sail.'

The information that he would shortly leave Liverpool, perhaps sail out of my life as swiftly as he had sailed in, was not pleasant. I was suddenly painfully aware of the U-boats sitting outside the Bay, reminded of the mourning women in the waiting room. I licked my lips and smiled up at him. 'I'll be here – but I may be late.'

'That's my girl,' he said more cheerfully and did a flamboyant, wild spin which would have made Norm wring his hands in horror had he spotted it.

'I don't know your name,' I ventured.

He laughed. 'God bless my soul! You don't, do you? Well, it's Harry O'Dwyer. And Doris said yours is Helen Forrester, right?'

'Yes,' I whispered. What was I doing? I must be crazy.

He whirled me into the corner reigned over by the collection of gold cups, and stopped. The last few bars of the music slowly trailed to an end, and Norm turned off the lights, except for the one over the gramophone table. He always said it was romantic to do so.

For a moment he held me close to him. It seemed to me that life had stopped, and he and I were suspended in a warm, cosy space of our own. Then, slowly he let go of me, and said, 'It's been a good evening, hasn't it?'

I came out of my trance, and agreed. 'It was fun.' With my hand still on his shoulder, I laughed softly, and asked, 'Before you go, tell me – where have we met before?'

'Don't you remember?'

'No.'

'Dear me. And I always thought I was such an unforgettable character!' He chuckled. 'Remember walking on Georges Landing Stage with an old man – your Dad, I imagine?'

Enlightment dawned. 'You were the man who kindly picked up my spectacles? And you wanted to meet me again – you said something about it earlier this evening? You really did?'

'Of course I did, dear, innocent, little Miss Helen,'

he mocked gently. He took my hand and led me over to the door, through the crowd making its way into the hall. He gave a small old-fashioned bow, and said, 'See you Tuesday.' He went away to join his friends and the crowd closed round him.

In a daze, I went to retrieve my shoes from the untidy pile in the big hall cupboard.

'My, my!' exclaimed Gloria, while she poked in the pile of shoes. 'You *have* made a conquest.'

I was offended, stood up straight suddenly and hit my head on the chin of a girl jostling me from behind. I apologised, and then said to Gloria, with a quiver in my voice, 'What nonsense! Me? I may have made a friend, Gloria.'

We crawled out between the pressing bodies, each with shoes in hand, and she said, as she wobbled on one foot while she put a shoe on the other one, 'Why not? Don't be upset. You're a proper nice girl – always said so. Keep yourself to yourself. And he's a fine looking fella.' She jabbed an elbow in my side, and added, 'Wish you luck, I do.'

Disarmed, I laughed self-consciously. 'Oh, Gloria.'

She giggled at me as, with shoes on, we straightened up. 'Lovely hair he's got.'

'Who's got lovely hair? Have I?' Her husband came from behind and put his arms round her waist, while I tried to remember what kind of hair Harry had.

'Not you, you old so-and-so,' she replied affectionately. 'You're going bald on top. That man Helen was dancing with.'

My face was scarlet. I heaved myself into my coat. I wanted to escape from their frank appraisal.

Her husband took his face away from its resting place on his wife's back, and gave her a push. 'Get away. You've got the girl all upset. She's as red as a beetroot.' He turned to me, his plain pasty face friendly. 'Don't take any notice of her. She's always looking for romances.'

I did my best to smile, but my lips were tight. I was nearly dead with embarrassment as I said, 'Good night,' and followed the crowd down the dark steps.

The blush slowly dissipated in the sharp September air, and I marched steadily home in the moonlight, trying to face the fact that the evening had been different from any evening I had ever spent – and that I could hardly wait until Tuesday. Common sense was saying, 'Don't be a fool. He's a sailor. Girls in every port. Experienced. And you're not much of a catch, despite Mother's efforts with clothes and things. Perhaps he won't even be there on Tuesday.'

Mother was still up when I arrived home, but I could not bring myself to tell her about the strange engineer. I feared her sarcastic tongue and the amused discussion that would probably go on behind my back. And suppose he did not come on Tuesday – I could not bear public humiliation. Mother, however, was anxious to discuss Fiona's latest escort. 'She's gone out to dinner at the George and then to dance,' she announced. 'He's a fully fledged General from the barracks. Said he saw her every morning waiting for the tram and had wanted to ask her for ages. So suitable, don't you think?'

'How exciting,' I responded absently, as I poured a cup of tea from the pot on the hob. I wondered if

Mother realised that Generals, usually men of good family, did not pick up girls from tram stops with any particularly honourable intention. I was anxious. Mother babbled on, however, and finally with no further comment I went to bed.

Probably Mother did not see Fiona's General in the same light that I did. She would think of him as an equal making himself known to an equal, a situation where he would tend to be much more careful of Fiona. I hoped wildly that Fiona was as big a prude as I thought her to be.

As I shivered in bed, I ticked myself off for being so stupid as to spend money on dancing, when what I really needed was a pair of thick blankets on my bed. I was as stupid as my mother, I upbraided myself. I determined to try to save up for this very expensive item, and the ache in my legs the next day reinforced the resolution. And then I remembered that if I bought a blanket, Mother would pawn it the first time she was short of money.

That week I cried for a city. Warsaw, brave, defiant old city, faced its final martyrdom, as German troops entered it. No point any more in trying to find its valiant voice on the radio. Another tragedy to add to that of the submarine, *Thetis*, which at that moment lay in Liverpool Bay while frantic efforts were made to raise her, though her crew were long since dead. In the office, my senior colleague faced not only supplicating hordes, but an ever growing pile of government instructions which had somehow to be read and understood and explained to our volunteer helpers. Her eyes were nearly as blackly ringed as mine. She scarcely stopped to eat and took a load of work home every night.

I often worked late at the office, but I never took work home. I could not face it. I walked a razor's edge. Though slowly recovering from years of privation, I was still by any normal standards in very poor health, still not well fed or properly warmed. Dancing had proved a real mental therapy but I tired easily. The war added its daily strain of perturbation. I worried about Alan and fretted about the children, though they were probably better looked after than if they were at home.

On Tuesday, as anticipated, I worked late. The trams taking me home seemed to crawl through the darkness. I ached with impatience. The house was in darkness, and I was greeted by an ecstatic dog and a note from Mother, who had thankfully gone to the cinema now it was open again. 'Gone to Rialto. Boil an egg.'

I duly boiled an egg, shared a slice of bread and margarine with the importuning dog, washed up a collection of dishes and made up the fire. It seemed as if invisible hands pulled at my skirt and made me slow. I washed carefully and then, holding the candle in my left hand, I made up my face. In its flickering light, I combed my curls softly round my face, peering anxiously into the piece of broken mirror wedged into the kitchen window. Would he be there?

Norm had left the front door unlatched, as he usually did on lesson nights, so I let myself in. I stood quietly in the big hall, shoes still dangling on my fingers, and stared through the open ballroom door.

He was there. Draped over a chair by the gramophone, if such a solid block of manhood could be said to be draped. He was talking to Norm. Neither man noticed my entrance, so I took a good look at him, and such a wild delight filled me that I wondered for a moment what was happening to me. Gloria was right. He did have nice hair of a nondescript fairness. He wore it a little longer than was the fashion. Without brilliantine, it curved comfortably round his forehead, a forehead which already had fine lines in it. Even relaxed, he radiated a considerable self-confidence. It was quiet, but it was there. It offered no direct threat, yet it suggested a powerful personality. Despite his easy manner and his light banter with me, he appeared a man not to be trifled with, either by a drunken seaman – or a flighty young woman.

I bit my lip, feeling hopelessly inadequate, and wondered if I should tiptoe out again. Where did he come from? Who were his people? His speech put him a cut above Norm's other customers, yet he was not what Father would have called a gentleman.

The sound of his hearty laugh rolled through the door, and plucking up courage, I changed my shoes and sidled in diffidently. I could already feel a blush rising up my neck. What was one supposed to say? How should I behave?

He had seen me. He immediately got up and came over and ushered me in. 'Hullo, little puss,' he said, and grinned all over his face, emphasising the lines on it.

He was so totally friendly that, as I opened my

handbag to pay Norm, I smiled back feeling more relaxed, and said, 'Hello.' He might call me little puss, but he himself was not unlike a dignified, amiable St Bernard dog. If he had had a tail I am sure it would have wagged in big, slow sweeps.

He put his hand over my bag and clipped it shut. 'It's fixed,' he assured me.

'Oh, but I can't . . . you can't,' I flustered. I looked appealingly at Norm, who assured me, 'Gentleman's privilege, luv.'

I swallowed, and said doubtfully, 'Well, thank you,' and allowed myself to be led to one of the chairs at the side of the ballroom, out of the way of the stumbling tango beginners. He sat down beside me, one arm curved along the back of my chair. 'I was afraid you weren't coming.'

I apologised for being late and said I hoped he had danced with someone else.

His response was scornful. 'With that bunch?'

'They're nice girls.'

He pursed up his mouth. 'Not my cup of tea.'

'Why do you come, then?'

'I came to please my landlord's wife last time. This time I came to see you.'

'Really and truly?' I smiled at him, flattered.

'Well, of course.' The gramophone struck up a quickstep. 'Would you like to dance?' he asked, unenthusiastically.

We danced. He was very quiet, and at the end he asked, 'Couldn't we go somewhere and get a cup of tea – and talk a while? There aren't any really nice places round here, but I know one which is very respectable.' He looked round the shabby, smoke-filled room. 'We'll never be able to talk much here – and I'm sailing Thursday night.'

I looked up sharply. I was suddenly afraid for him. Fear must have shown on my face, because he said, 'Don't be scared. I'll take good care of you. Ask Norm – he's known me off and on for a long time.'

'Mother will be expecting me home soon after eleven,' I dithered, while my pulses beat madly.

'I'll get you home in time. Promise.'

He looked so wistful and inside me was stirring a crazy pleasure at being singled out by him. 'Please, little Miss Helen.'

'I'll get my coat and shoes,' I said, trembling inwardly.

Chapter thirty

We sat down opposite each other in a steamy little café. We were the only customers. A fat, white-aproned woman stood behind a small counter laden with two hissing gas rings with bubbling kettles on them. An assortment of plates covered with glass domes held sandwiches and buns. The woman came over to our plain deal table, and said, ''lo, Harry, me luv, what is it tonight?'

Harry looked inquiringly at me, and I said primly, 'A cup of tea would be very nice.'

Harry ordered two teas.

'Would your young lady like something to eat? I've got some fresh bath buns – or you could have something hot?'

I was, as usual, hungry, but I had no idea of his financial situation, so I said with a smile at the friendly soul waiting in front of us, that a bun would be lovely. His young lady, indeed!

Harry was grinning at me like a small boy. He nodded towards the retreating female. 'Come here for years for most of my meals, when I'm ashore. It's quiet. Jack's wife gives me breakfast – I eat my other meals out, so as not to intrude on them. He's First Mate, and it's like a permanent honeymoon there when he's home. Ma here keeps me well fed, don't you, Ma?' He looked across at the counter, where a large pot of tea was in the making. Ma looked up and smiled and said she did her best.

'Why do you have to work so late?' he asked, stirring two spoonfuls of sugar into the cup of tea I had poured for him. I bit into the huge bun brought me on a thick white plate. 'It's the sinking of the *Athenia* and the *Courageous*. Every boat that goes to sea seems to have Bootle men on it – and we're looking after their widows.' Then I remembered, as his face sobered, that he went to sea, too, so I added hastily, 'I'm sorry, I should not have mentioned it.'

He sighed heavily, and put his elbows on the table and clasped his hands, big well-shaped hands with scarred knuckles and very short nails, broken in places.

'That's all right,' he said and was quiet, biting absently on his knuckles. 'I'm a Bootle man myself. My Mum and Dad still live there. Dad's retired. He went to sea – ship's purser.'

'You don't stay with them?' I inquired, guardedly.

'No.' He appeared to be cogitating over the question and continued to chew his knuckles. 'I'm too old to be bothering them now. I got used to living away from them – for a while Mam wouldn't have such a limb of Satan over the doorstep.'

'What?' Despite a mouthful of glutinous bun, I had to laugh.

'It's true,' he said ruefully. 'She's still a bit edgy with me.'

Still laughing, I asked, 'Whatever did you do to offend her so?'

'Decided I'd never make a priest – so I went over the wall.'

It was a totally unexpected answer, and I stared at him in astonishment. 'Really? A priest?'

'Yes. Why not?'

I nodded. Why not? So many Catholic families hoped to have one child enter the church, either as a priest or nun. The child would be brain-washed almost from infancy, so that it would never consider doing anything else. But this was the first rebel I had ever met – or even heard of.

'Did you study for it?'

'Yes. At first I thought I'd make it. Then it was as if part of me was dying inside. Don't know how to explain it. Like being slowly strangled, if you under-stand.' He was spreading out a watery ring on the table, and the blue eyes glanced up at me, as if to judge how I was taking his admission. 'I guess I didn't have the necessary discipline.'

'What did your teachers do?'

'Oh, them. They were very good. They made me mull it over good and plenty – because it costs money to educate a priest – and I think some of them really cared. But they don't want discontented men, and finally I left – with their blessing. They did it without making me feel guilty. But my Mum – that was a different matter.'

'What about your father?'

'Oh, he's a real old philosopher. Nothing gets him. But he does what Mum says while he's home. He's got to live with her! Neither of them takes kindly to him being home all the time. She's used to running the place – because of him being at sea all the time.'

I had seen enough seamen's wives to understand

253

the matriarchal set-up. 'So what did you do?' I asked.

'Never even unpacked after I came home from the seminary. Got shown the door. God, she was furious. I went to stay with my married brother for a day or two. Then I got a job sweeping out a warehouse. I didn't know what to do – jobs are as scarce as hens' teeth. Then I met a pal – a lad I'd known at school – and he got me a job with him aboard a miserable little tub – Goddam awful boat – excuse the language – and I was as sick as a dog the first week. It was rough – my God, it was. But having a pal aboard a bit older than me made all the difference – saved me from the worst, till I got to know the ropes.'

'Are you always sick?' I asked. I wondered with dim horror what the worst was. All the seamen I had ever interviewed spoke of vermin, poor food and low wages.

'No. Never been sick since, oddly enough.' He smiled at my empty plate, and signalled Ma to bring another bun.

'Don't you go to see your mother?'

He sighed. 'Yeah. But she's never forgiven me and never lets me forget it. So I don't go every time I'm ashore. I give her a little allotment, so that if ever I stop one she'd get a bit of a pension. See my dad more often and my brother.'

I looked at the old, young face in front of me, the openness and geniality of it, and wondered how any woman could be bitter enough to show a son like that to the door.

'Your mother doesn't realise what she is missing,' I said impulsively.

'Och, you're a sweetheart,' he said with sudden cheerfulness, and drank up his tea.

'Being used to study must have helped you pass your exams to be an engineer – though it is so very different.'

'Well, I had to start from scratch. But grammar school is a good place for learning to learn – and the Fathers at the seminary certainly reinforced it. They wouldn't have any backsliding. You can learn anything if you're really set on it.'

The room was hot, and he opened his navy blue jacket, to show a creased waistcoat with a watch chain across it. He also wore a wrist watch with an expanding gilt band. Inwardly I smiled at the creases on the waistcoat. I could not remember seeing a merchant seaman whose clothes were properly pressed. I suppose, if they took them to sea, they kept them rolled up. And this man had no one to look after him ashore. He picked up the conversation again, and continued, 'I don't drink, except the odd glass of wine – tried as a youngster, of course, and threw up a good many times before I gave up. So I've time to read – makes you a bit cut off from your mates at times – and I saved – so it was easy for me to take time out for Courses.'

'It's unusual for a seaman not to drink. I thought they all *lived* on rum, more or less.'

He laughed. 'Get away. There's always a few that don't. My father never did.'

'Well, what do you do when you're in a strange place?'

'Sometimes there's a Sailors' Home or some place,

255

where you can get a game of billiards – or you can go to a show or a match or into the bazaars. There's another chap, a Methodist, and he doesn't drink either, so we sometimes go together.' He looked at me slyly, and added, 'Pick up a girl occasionally.'

'Do you consider that you picked up me?' I asked tartly.

He grinned, hesitated, and then said, 'No. I hope I've made a permanent acquisition.'

I was so happy that I simply glowed. It must have been obvious to him, because he caught my hand across the table and gave it a hearty squeeze. For a moment we were united, and then bashfully I withdrew my hand, and asked shyly, 'What else do you do?'

'Well, not a great deal. Often enough, you're too busy to have much time ashore. I read a lot – take a pile of books with me. Get fed up at times – particularly not having a home to go to.' He lit a cigarette and blew a neat smoke ring into the air. 'Enough of this old man. How about you?'

This was a question I had been dreading. What should I tell him? How could I explain my odd parents? If I explained my origins, would he think I was swanking and despise me?

My unease must have shown on my face, because he said gently, 'It doesn't matter, luv. I can see you've had a bad time – it's written all over you.' Then he leaned forward and took my hand again. 'I don't care what you are – or anything. I know a good thing when I see it. I did when I picked your specs up off Georges Landing.'

He astonished me. Did I really show what had happened to me? Or what did he think I was – something dreadful? I sat looking down at my hands clasped over my handbag on my knee. I had to acknowledge an overwhelming desire to keep his interest, and was mortally afraid of not being able to do it. I wanted so much that he should think well of me.

He was sitting, elbows on table, a long ash on his cigarette, as quietly as if he were waiting for a badger to emerge from its burrow in the evening light.

The silence between us continued, until he began to smile at me, and as if to help me, began to talk again.

'You know, a man in my position doesn't often get the chance of meeting a decent woman like you – unless you strike lucky. When you don't have a home base, you can be cut off, like. And when you start out to be a priest, you try not to think about women – in that kind of way, if you know what I mean,' he muddled on, going a bit pink himself.

I smiled back at him. 'Yes, I understand. You wouldn't be taking out the girls who lived near you – the ones you'd normally meet – when you were in your teens, for example.'

He chuckled. 'Right.'

Suddenly I felt more at ease. 'Well,' I said, 'I've been cut off in a way, too.'

He looked at his wrist watch. 'Do you feel like walking home?'

I nodded agreement, and he signalled to Ma. She eased herself round the counter and he paid her. With his money in her red hand, she smiled down at me in a most approving way, and winked at Harry. I blushed yet again, and, as I rose, I thanked her.

Harry ushered me through the narrow door of the café and somehow his arm stayed round my waist as we slowly walked up the hill. He had a sailor's eyesight and steered me safely in the dark, overcast night. The whole city seemed still.

'Tell me how you came to be cut off, too,' he demanded.

It was easier talking in the dark, to a comfortable, warm presence strolling by me. A man I felt to be honest deserved honesty, so slowly, sometimes with pain, I told him what had happened to our family and its consequences to me.

He heard me through, with only an occasional exclamation. As we neared our street, I fell silent. What is he going to think of such a crazy family? I wondered. So unbalanced, not established, unpredictable except in their stupidity.

'You poor kid,' he said compassionately, and tightened his arm round my waist.

At the top of our road, he stopped and turned me to him. He paused, as if considering something for a moment, and then very carefully kissed me on the cheek. 'What's your office phone number?' he asked. 'I'll be busy now. Won't be able to see you until we dock again. I'll phone you as soon as I'm back – and we'll make a proper date. Officially, I'm not supposed to know where we're going – allow five weeks. O.K.?'

I was trembling in his confining arms, with a scarifying, overwhelmingly strange feeling within me.

'Yes,' I whispered.

'Which is your house?' he asked.

'It's the seventh – no, the eighth – down on this side.'

'Right. Just in case I can't get you on the phone, I'll know where to find you.'

'Do you have an address?' I asked nervously, trying to sound normal when I felt far from normal.

He immediately gave me the address of his lodgings. I wanted instinctively to put my arms around him and beg him not to go, but I was too shy.

A number of short voyages and happy reunions later, he told me that to gain my full confidence was harder than making friends with the disillusioned ship's cat, who regarded the cook as his sole friend, and then persuading the beast to come on to his lap.

Chapter thirty-one

Five weeks seemed an interminable time. When the thirty-five days were over and there was no telephone call I was nearly distracted. Harry had told me the name of his ship, and certainly no one had come into the office to claim a pension because the ship was lost – in those days of official silence about the total number of our losses, this was the most likely way I would have known if it had gone to the bottom.

On the forty-first day I could bear it no longer, and with elaborate casualness I asked Norm if he had heard anything.

Norm dusted one of his records, and said that almost certainly if Harry's pal from the same ship was missing, he would have heard about it – so the ship was still afloat. If it had docked, Jack's wife nagged him so much to be taken dancing that they would have been in the room that minute. He grinned knowingly at me. 'He's a proper nice lad, isn't he? I knew you'd like him.'

I nodded and smiled – and sighed.

'Don't you worry, luv. He'll be back like a homing pigeon. He needs a girl like you.'

But I did worry. Something wonderful, something precious, had plunged light-heartedly into my miserable existence, and I could not bear to lose it. I knew of so many little ships limping home damaged, or lost at sea. I realised to the full what many of the stony-faced women who came to our office for advice were going through.

Fiona, secretive and sour-faced, announced to Mother's disappointment that she did not like her General and had dropped him. Fiona had more sense than she was ever given credit for.

She stayed at home one night and set my hair for me. I was tempted to tell her about Harry. Yet, as she chatted on about films she had seen and dances she had been to, I thought better of it. Surrogate Mums listen; they are not expected to have anything to confide. Secretly, I dreaded ever having to introduce a man friend to Fiona. Her charm, her sex appeal, were overwhelming, like Mother's in her younger days. I would not stand a dog's chance against such competition.

Mother was fretting over a Government demand that parents contribute towards the billeting allowance made to the hosts of evacuees. The sum suggested was six shillings for each child, a little over half the allowance. Both parents grumbled that they could not afford it, though they could now afford to smoke, to drink, to attend the cinema or concerts. They had grown used to having money in their pockets, as I had with my little allowance.

I dreaded being returned to my earlier impossible penury, and I again advertised for a shorthand student, still without result. I had continued to apply for jobs advertised in the *Liverpool Echo*.

Unemployment was still very high, and employers could obtain stenographers who had matriculated.

Few of the men who interviewed me bothered to examine the sheaf of certificates which I had received for my night school endeavours. I was also still very poorly dressed in comparison with other girls who worked in offices, though I had now taught myself to make and alter underwear and dresses quite successfully. Not that I had the use of what I made for very long. All too frequently painstakingly hand-stitched petticoats and renovated dresses were borrowed by plumper Mother and Fiona, to be left dirty and with seams burst. I raged impotently and tried hiding my single change of underwear under the mattress. To no avail. I was a rotten, greedy bad-tempered daughter and sister who did not trust her relations. My despair about Harry did not improve my patience.

Another worry was that Mother began to justify avoiding paying the billeting charges for the children, by saying her darlings must be homesick and want to return. It certainly would have been cheaper to have them at home, because the price of food was still low – and we did not eat well anyway.

I brought a storm of recrimination down on my head by reminding Mother that, though Liverpool had not yet been bombed, there was no guarantee that it would not be soon. I wondered bitterly how much real affection she had for her children; she did not seem to really miss them very much. This idea strengthened my mistrust of Mother, despite her keeping her word to me regarding her share of my salary. I found myself even less able to talk to her, except for common courtesies.

After forty-two days I gave up. Either Harry's ship

was lost, or he had abandoned the clumsy hobble-dehoy he had picked up. Probably the latter, I told myself acidly. Moodily I slammed files on to shelves, typed letters and was sent out to visit invalids or the elderly, who were always remarkably sweet to me.

'Miss Forrester,' called my colleague, holding up our solitary telephone. 'A call for you. Make it quick, because I have a lot of phoning to do.'

I blenched with the surprise of it, and almost snatched the instrument from her, 'Hello,' I murmured.

'Little Miss Forrester?'

'Yes.'

'Harry here. Look, sweetheart. We've just berthed. It's going to be a quick turnaround this time. Could you meet me at Mrs Ambleton's place – you know, the little café we went to – tonight, seven-thirty, eh?'

'Yes,' I breathed. 'Oh, yes, of course.'

'Wait for me if I'm late?'

'Yes.'

'I'll be there. 'Bye.' The phone clicked as he rang off.

In a dream I handed the receiver back to my intrigued colleague, who was smiling questioningly at me. 'Thank you,' I said, and then added, 'I'll check how the waiting room is doing.' And I fled, down to the unused basement of the house which was our office, pushed open a creaking door into an old kitchen wreathed with cobwebs, shut myself in, and burst into tears with relief.

Chapter thirty-two

While my colleague was out visiting a difficult case, I made a fast call to Fiona and asked her to tell Mother I would not be in for tea. 'We'll be sending out for some sandwiches to eat in the office while we work,' I lied merrily. Fiona had obviously been expecting a call from someone else, because her lively 'Hello' turned to 'What, you?' when she heard my voice. She promised, however, to relay the message.

'Where's Harry?' asked Ma through a cloud of steam from her kettles.

'He's coming,' I puffed, as I took off my darned woollen gloves and loosened my coat.

'Like a coop o' tea while you're waiting, luv?'

'Yes, please.' My eyes were on the narrow door. I was dreadfully hungry, but I was so happy, so wonderfully, wonderfully happy.

Eight o'clock came and went, and slowly my hopes shrivelled. Three men went out, and a man and a girl came in and sat down to a meal. The smell of sausages was tantalising.

He came in slowly and, for a moment, until his crumpled face broke into a lively grin, I hardly recognised him. He was dressed in beige twill cotton trousers, a blue shirt open at the neck, worn under an open black leather jacket. His face was almost without colour, except for red rings round eyes so weary I wondered how they stayed open. In one hand he carried a flat white paper bag. He came towards me eagerly, whipping off a navy blue peaked sailor's cap, as he approached.

'Eh, I'm that glad to see you,' he said, putting his arm round my shoulder for a second, before turning to swing into the chair opposite me. 'Thought I'd never get loose. How are you, luv?'

I was all curled up inside with pure joy. I wanted to hug him, and I am sure my face glowed, as I said, 'Oh, I'm all right. What about you?'

He looked exhausted, as if he should have been in bed, instead of meeting a stray girl in a café; and my happiness flowed out in compassion for him.

He grinned, and said, 'Well, I'm starving. Have you had your tea?'

I nodded negatively while my eyes dwelt on him, and he called to the beaming, fat lady, 'What have you got, Nell?'

She offered steak and kidney pie or sausage and mash, with steamed treacle pudding to follow.

Over a huge helping of pie, I repeated my question, 'What about you? You look worn out.'

'Been chasing all over the bloody Atlantic, if you'll pardon the language.' He began to eat quickly, as if he were indeed starving. 'Convoy got scattered – it was slow as a company of snails, anyway. We made it home on our own – we're fast compared to most freighters.'

A shiver of dread went through me. I refrained, however, from asking any more questions. Time enough to talk when he had eaten his dinner and unwound a little.

Between mouthfuls, I kept glancing up at him, amazed that he had thought of me first when he came ashore, that he really was sitting opposite me.

He caught my questing eye. 'Never stopped thinkin' about you,' he said, with a piece of kidney balanced neatly on his fork.

The tell-tale flush flooded my face. I wanted to say, 'I never stopped thinking of you.' But I was too proud to commit myself. This kind, comfortable man might soon get fed up with my long silences and my gauche ways.

'I'm so glad you got back safe,' I finally managed, a bit primly.

He leaned back and laughed. 'Wasn't too bad, luv. I was thankful to see Blackpool Tower, though, I can tell you.'

I thought about the sea mines being laid by both combatants, of surface raiders, of the dreaded U-boats, as yet only flexing their muscles. Suddenly I felt the icy Atlantic waters with its surface mist drifting over struggling men. I felt the choking water in my own lungs, and I asked impulsively in a strangled voice, 'Do you have to do another voyage? Can't you stay ashore – do something else?'

His eyes were intent on me, speculative. 'No, little Helen. We all have to go back. Even if I decided to swallow the anchor – and I might – I can't do it until this little ruckus is over. What about some pudding?'

I tried to console myself with a piece of steamed pudding big enough for a hungry lorry driver.

Steamed pudding did not help much. I was in love. I knew it. In love with someone I was seeing for only the third time. It was ridiculous, absurd, stupid, certainly unwise. Then I told myself piteously that there was no harm in loving, as long as one did not expect anything in return. As always with the children, perhaps I could give him love without consideration of what I would get out of it. Physical love I would have to be careful about, but that was only part of it – it was the commitment which mattered.

I need not have worried about being left with an infant to care for. I was dealing with a most unusual man, who, however he felt, was very much in command of himself. It was almost disappointing not to have to fight for one's honour.

We spent the rest of the evening riding backwards and forwards on the ferry boat, crossing and recrossing the Mersey river. Tucked in the curve of Harry's arm, it was a good place to talk and get to know each other.

On the first trip, he put the white paper bag on my lap. 'I brought you a present,' he announced.

Surprised, I picked up the bag hesitantly. 'May I look?'

He nodded expectantly, and I opened the bag, touched material and carefully drew it out.

It was a dress, and I did not need to totally unfold it to know that it was a very good dress. The colour in the poor light was either tan or dark red. It had tiny pin tucks running the length of the bodice on which was pinned a discreet leather flower touched with gold. It had long sleeves, and could, I guessed, be worn for any occasion.

'Harry!' I exclaimed, blushing. 'It is too – too

much – you should not have done it – but, oh, it's beautiful. Thank you very much.'

His arm tightened round me. 'Didn't know your vital statistics, but I found a girl the same size, I think. Like it?'

I shook it out and admired its fine leather belt, its plain skirt, and turned starry eyes up to him. 'It's perfect,' I said. 'I've never had anything so beautiful before.'

Our faces were very close together and I thought he would kiss me, but he didn't. Just hugged me tighter.

'Thought you'd like it. Went down to the garment district in Manhattan and looked around. My pal often buys things there for his wife. They've got everything there – stuff that goes to the good shops.'

I was overwhelmed. 'You shouldn't spend so much on me,' I protested.

'Humph. And who else would I be spending it on? That's the trouble with me. Never had anybody I wanted to buy presents for, for years.'

I laughed, and carefully folded up the dress and put it back into the bag. How I was going to explain it to Mother and Fiona or stop them from borrowing it, I had no idea. I could not explain my happy acceptance of it even to myself – and from a Roman Catholic, to boot.

We sat talking together, warm and happy, two odd, extremely lonely people, neither of whom had had very much out of life except work, and yet matched like a pair of gloves. I wondered what had happened to my passionate belief in my church, feelings strong enough to make me refuse confirmation from a church which demanded that its members go to Confession.

This remembrance made me turn to him and snuggling close, say, 'Harry, I have to tell you – you know, I'm a Protestant.'

He chuckled unexpectedly. 'I thought so. Do you feel very strongly about it?'

'I'm not sure. I used to feel that no other religion was a true one. But the more I see the more I realise that nobody can really say that.'

'Well, not to worry, my dear. Times they are a-changing. We'll talk about it some more another day.'

Nevertheless, we continued to talk about beliefs, though not very deeply, and then about ships' engines – very deeply and far out of my depth. Finally, we came round to the war, which was always at the back of everybody's mind, and in this regard Harry said, 'Y' know, I've never been out of work since I went to sea – and I've saved. Since the war began I've been getting danger money – and it is going to add up. So I was thinkin' of buying a house – I know it sounds daft – but I'm fed up with not having a place of my own. I want a decent place and I've been bickering with a chap out at Allerton who's got a few new houses for sale. Would you like to come sometime and look at one with me?'

I was a bit staggered, and my mind leaped ahead with all kinds of wild hopes. Remember, I told myself, don't expect anything. 'I'd love to,' I assured him. 'It must be miserable not having a home.'

'It is,' he said, looking at me positively wickedly.

To be able to buy a house – to have the money to do it – seemed to me an almost impossible ambition. Presumably, however, he knew what he was doing.

'When do you sail again?'

'Couple of days,' he replied soberly. 'Real quick turn around. Never know what they'll do next. They're even shifting crews around to other companies, as if they were ruddy pawns.'

'It's happening ashore, too,' I said.

He eased himself around, in order to look at me directly, 'Like to come dancing tomorrow night? I can get loose for a few hours – they owe me plenty. We can go to the Rialto, if you like.'

'Let's go to Norm's,' I suggested. The Rialto seemed suddenly a cold and alien place.

'Okay, and I'll try to think of a nice place for coffee afterwards.'

He said he would get the overhead railway back to the dock, and saw me on to the tram with only a gentle peck on my cheek. It was very disappointing. He told me later that he was so afraid of scaring me off and yet his time ashore was so little.

I did not have to account for the new dress, because everyone was in bed when I arrived home, and the next morning they all rushed off to work without remembering that they had not seen me the previous evening. While Fiona was washing herself in the kitchen, I hid the pretty garment on a hanger under my old brown winter coat, which was by this time too decrepit even to be pawned and was sometimes used as a bed cover.

I tore home that evening and shared tea with Mother and Fiona, because Father was working late. It was unusual for me to lie, but that night I lied like the proverbial trooper. I said I had bought a new dress from a well-known second hand shop which dealt in high class clothing, and was going to press it to wear to the dance club that evening.

When Fiona saw it, her eyes widened. 'You lucky thing!' she exclaimed. 'Do you think they'd have anything to fit me?'

'Probably they would,' I responded non-committally, as I carefully ran the flat iron over it on the kitchen table. To press such a garment without an ironing board was a skill learned from patient experiment.

It was a tan shade which suited my sallow complexion, and it fitted very well, too well, I hoped, for either Fiona or Mother to get into it. 'It *is* a nice dress, more like an American fashion than an English one,' Mother said quite innocently, leaving me tight-lipped and silent. 'You should go and have a look, Fiona, and see what they have.'

I could imagine what Mother would say if she knew a man had given it to me, and particularly if later that man dropped me. I could not face such humiliation. The less said the less humiliation there would be.

He was there, waiting for me, joking with Norm and Doris, all dressed up in creased navy blue. He whistled when he saw me. I had not been able to see myself in the dress, because we lacked a long mirror.

Doris said, 'Golly, you look nice, Helen!'

I looked across at myself in the long ballroom mirror and knew that I looked good. And I felt good, more sure of myself. The girl in the mirror was much as I had imagined myself growing up to be, if disaster had not struck the family first. I had agonised over having to wear black shoes and carry a black handbag with a tan dress, but they were an elegant contrast.

We danced and we danced until the end of the evening, oblivious of anyone else. He looked less weary and I was so happy.

Afterwards, five or six of us stood in the misty moonlight outside the front door, chatting casually. I was carrying my walking shoes, meaning to go home in my dancing shoes. Harry offered to put the shoes in his raincoat pocket – there was no doubt that I was going to be escorted home this time.

One of the girls laughed, looking at my satin-clad feet. 'Goin' to dance home?' she asked.

'I could dance all night,' I replied lightly, glancing up at Harry. 'I could dance the length of the avenue.'

'Get away, now.'

I laughed. 'Bet I could.'

'Bet *we* could,' said Harry, joining in the laughter, and he put his arm round me and, whistling a slow waltz, he turned me away from the cheerful little group, and we danced away down the pavement.

I was shyly quiet in the warmth of his arms. The other young people called, 'Tara, well. Enjoy yourselves,' and their voices faded as they walked in the other direction.

'I'd like you to meet some of my friends,' Harry remarked, as we danced to our own peculiar music

272

down the empty avenue. 'I've a few old friends, mostly married, round Bootle.'

'I'd like that very much,' I said.

'We'll do it next time I'm home. They're more like your kind of people than that bunch are.'

I was no longer sure what my kind of people were, so I did not answer. But I felt that any friend of his was likely to be pleasant to know.

Only the sound of our shifting feet broke the silence. I was afloat in happiness. There was no beginning to life and no end, only the perfect now in the arms of a semi-stranger who meant everything to me, a stranger who was already planning to introduce me to his friends, take me into his life.

Half-way down the avenue he stopped, and holding me tightly, lifted my face and kissed me, a kind of kiss I had never imagined and I never wanted to stop. But he did stop it with a quick sigh, and a resumption of our slow progress, while all kinds of wild and wonderful feelings raced through my slender body.

'Love, I know this is too quick. But I want to marry you, if you'll have me – soon as I can get a house ready to put you in safe and sound.' He ignored my gasp, and went on, 'I'm askin' you now, because I'm away so much that I could lose you to somebody else.'

I was struck dumb, and he urged, as he stopped dancing again, 'Be my girl – I'll never let you down, I promise. I've always wanted a wife like you – someone I could really talk to – and so pretty.'

'Are you sure, Harry?'

He laughed. 'I know a good thing when I see it.'

'Then, of course, I will. I can't think of anything

I would like better. And I'll try to be a good wife – I know how to keep house – and, oh, Harry, I want to make you happy.'

Instinctively, I lifted my hand from his shoulder and touched the tired face, and whispered, 'I love you.'

'My girl – my little Miss Helen!' He swung me off my feet in a happy whirl, and then we went on dancing, dancing down the avenue into the Liverpool mist.

March 1950

March 1950

'Goodness me!' exclaimed Mother. 'What have you got there?' She looked askance at me, as I staggered through the kitchen door into the marshy back garden, with a huge drawer from the dresser in my bedroom. The drawer was stacked with papers, some of them in neatly tied bundles.

'It's all the letters I received during the war – all my love letters, too. I can't very well take them to India, so I thought I would burn them in the old bomb crater in the garden.'

I must have looked a little stricken, because Mother said very kindly, 'Yes, dear. Burn the lot. India is going to be an entirely new start for you.' Age had mellowed her a little and I was grateful for her quick sympathy, though she was still very difficult to live with.

Father looked up from his paper sadly. He did not want me to go so far away. He hoped my fiancé would find a post in England and that we would return soon. He was a much plumper and better dressed father now, and in good health. We had become friends and we would miss each other.

I thankfully dropped the drawer on the dew-spangled grass in the bomb crater, and stood panting with the effort of lifting it. Across the flat market gardens at the bottom of our land, I could see the sea wall which protected the district from becoming fenland again. It was dull mist-covered country, but I felt it was my country, because it was so close to where my grandmother had lived. Behind me stood the small, though pleasantly comfortable, bungalow which had sheltered us since 1941, when a bomb had made our Liverpool row house unsafe. The grass-covered crater at my feet had been caused by a small bomb which had fallen on our first night in our new home. Now in March, 1950, I proposed to incinerate in it the record of all my past life. Before me stretched a brand new path, totally unrelated to all that had gone before. I was going out to India to marry a gentle Hindu professor of Theoretical Physics, whom I had met in Liverpool when he was taking a doctoral degree at the university.

How strange life was. I was to give up a very promising career, take on a new country, a new religion, a new language, for this quiet person who had come into my life so unobtrusively that it was some time before I really noticed that he was there. And yet I was content, happy about it.

I crumpled up some newspaper which I had brought into the bomb crater, and set a match to it. Then one by one I opened out and dropped into the flames letters from all over the world from my three brothers, Alan, Brian and Tony, all of whom had served in the war and come home safely. They were now launched on new careers, determined to make up for the time lost. No letters from Baby Edward. He was now ensconced in Liverpool University on a scholarship. He had been kept out of the Forces by an untreated dislocated shoulder caused by a fall in childhood. Letters followed from umpteen men who had danced with me, taken me out, in some cases proposed to me, while like a lost soul I had searched frantically to find someone like Harry. But no one can take the place of somebody else. They have to be loved in their own right. I knew that now, but it had taken me a long time to learn it.

Here it was, a little clipping from the *Liverpool Echo*, with his picture: 'O'Dwyer – Henry, aged 33, lost at sea, beloved son of Maureen and John O'Dwyer, and loving brother of Thomas and sister-in-law Dorothy. RIP.'

It was as if the flames were burning part of me.

Woodenly, I continued to throw letters on the fire. Very few letters from women. My girl friends had been fortunate, like me, in spending the war at home. None from Fiona, just married and living close by, or from Avril, who was still living at home. Avril was taking the first uncertain steps which would eventually lead her to a full and satisfying teaching career, to marriage and four bonny children.

A form letter from the Petroleum Board offering me a post at £2 14s 6d a week – three times my salary in the charitable organisation. How I had leaped at it. A living wage at last.

I started on a packet of letters tied with blue baby ribbon and, half choked with smoke and misery, threw them one by one on to the fire. Dear, highly articulate Edward, six feet tall and built to it, had taken nearly two hours to propose to me, while marching along the road to Birkenhead Park station, when he had missed the local train home and I had

279

decided to walk part of the way with him. It had taken me only ten seconds to accept.

Half-way through I could not continue. I snatched some of the letters back and have them still, a tiny bundle with another obituary culled from the *Liverpool Echo*. 'Parry – July – killed in action, aged 32 years, Edward, very dearly loved younger son of Mrs Parry, Orrell Park, his loving and sorrowing mother.'

That was 1944 – the invasion of France. I thought I was a Jonah, so after the war I concentrated on finding a career and discovered it in a packaging company, where women had a chance to rise in the business. I joined all kinds of social clubs and societies and made a number of good friends.

Now I live in western Canada with my dear Professor and our son. As I write, it is the beginning of 1981, and I have trunks full of letters, a much, much happier collection. Pictures of Fiona's and Avril's beautiful weddings, and those of the boys – what funny hats we wore; snaps of a dozen or more nephews and nieces; letters from my publishers accepting the manuscripts of *Twopence to Cross the Mersey* and *Minerva's Stepchild*,* in which I described the sufferings of our family when we first came to Liverpool; lovely letters from my kind Indian in-laws. And my husband's long letters written to me from India before I went there and others from time to time when he has been away from me for a few days. How much I owe him for making my life anew. We came out to this wealthy, snowy country so that he could better continue his research, and here was born our son.

My cup runneth over.

*Published in Fontana as *Liverpool Miss*.

Helen Forrester

LIVERPOOL MISS

The continuing story of Helen Forrester's poverty-stricken childhood in Liverpool during the Depression. The Forrester family are slowly winning their fight for survival. But fourteen-year-old Helen's personal battle is to persuade her parents to allow her to earn her own living, to lead her own life after the years of neglect and inadequate schooling while she cared for her six younger brothers and sisters. Her untiring struggles against illness, caused by severe malnutrition, dirt (she has her first bath in four years), and above all the selfish demands of her parents, make this true story of courage and perseverance heart-breaking yet heart-warming.

'Records of hardship during the Thirties or earlier are not rare; but this has features that make it stand apart' – *Observer*

'An impressive record of what it is like to be very poor . . . written with a simplicity which is moving and memorable' – *Homes and Gardens*

'The story of a young girl's courage and perseverance against adversity . . . warm-hearted and excellent' – *Manchester Evening News*

Helen Forrester

TWOPENCE TO CROSS
THE MERSEY

Helen Forrester tells the sad but never sentimental story of her childhood years, during which her family fell from genteel poverty to total destitution. In the depth of the Depression, mistakenly believing that work would be easier to find, they moved from the South of England to the slums of Liverpool. Here Helen Forrester, the eldest of seven children, experienced the worst degradations that being poor can bring. She writes about them without self-pity but rather with a rich sense of humour which makes her account of these grim days before the Welfare State funny as well as painful.

'The clarity with which utter privation is here recorded is of a rare kind' – Gillian Reynolds, *Guardian*

'. . . records, with remarkable steadiness and freedom from self-pity, the story of a childhood that – even if it was all forty years ago – most people would have set down in rage and despair' – Edward Blishen, *Books and Bookmen*

'. . . her restraint and humour in describing this stark history make it all the more moving' – *Daily Telegraph*

Helen Forrester

Twopence to Cross the Mersey
Liverpool Miss
By the Waters of Liverpool

– the three volumes of her autobiography –

Helen Forrester tells the sad but never sentimental story of
her childhood years, during which her family fell from
genteel poverty to total destitution. In the depth of the
Depression, mistakenly believing that work would be
easier to find, they moved from the South of England to the
slums of Liverpool. The family slowly win their fight for
survival, but Helen's personal battle was to persuade her
parents to allow her to earn her own living, and to lead her
own life after the years of neglect and inadequate schooling
while she cared for her six younger brothers and sisters.
Illness, caused by severe malnutrition, dirt, and above all
the selfish demands of her parents, make this a story of
courage and perseverance. She writes without self-pity but
rather with a rich sense of humour which makes her
account of these grim days before the Welfare State funny
as well as painful.

'Records of hardship during the Thirties are not rare; but
this has features that make it stand apart' *Observer*

FONTANA PAPERBACKS

Rhanna
Christine Marion Fraser

A rich, romantic, Scottish saga set
on the Hebridean island of Rhanna

Rhanna

The poignant story of life on the rugged and tranquil island
of Rhanna, and of the close-knit community for whom it
is home.

Rhanna at War

Rhanna's lonely beauty is no protection against the horrors
of war. But Shona Mackenzie, home on leave, discovers
that the fiercest battles are those between lovers.

Children of Rhanna

The four island children, inseparable since childhood, find
that growing up also means growing apart.

Return to Rhanna

Shona and Niall Mackenzie come home to find Rhanna
unspoilt by the onslaught of tourism. But then tragedy
strikes at the heart of their marriage.

Song of Rhanna

Ruth is happily married to Lorn. But the return to Rhanna
of her now famous friend Rachel threatens Ruth's
happiness.

'Full-blooded romance, a strong, authentic setting'
Scotsman

FONTANA PAPERBACKS

Book Tokens

**Give them
the pleasure of choosing**

Book Tokens can be bought
and exchanged at most
bookshops.

Fontana Paperbacks: Non-fiction

Fontana is a leading paperback publisher of non-fiction, both popular and academic.

- ☐ Street Fighting Years *Tariq Ali* £3.95
- ☐ The Boys and the Butterflies *James Birdsall* £3.95
- ☐ Time and Chance *James Callaghan* £5.95
- ☐ Jane Fonda *Michael Freedland* £3.95
- ☐ Perestroika *Mikhail Gorbachev* £3.95
- ☐ The Real Charles *Alan Hamilton* £3.95
- ☐ Going For It! *Victor Kiam* £3.95
- ☐ Keep Going For It! *Victor Kiam* £3.50
- ☐ In the Name of the Working Class *Sandor Kopacsi* £3.95
- ☐ Lucan: Not Guilty *Sally Moore* £3.95
- ☐ Yamani *Jeffrey Robinson* £3.95
- ☐ Don't Ask the Price *Marcus Sieff* £3.95
- ☐ Nor Iron Bars a Cage *Penelope Tremayne* £3.95
- ☐ Just Williams *Kenneth Williams* £2.95

You can buy Fontana paperbacks at your local bookshop or newsagent. Or you can order them from Fontana Paperbacks, Cash Sales Department, Box 29, Douglas, Isle of Man. Please send a cheque, postal or money order (not currency) worth the purchase price plus 22p per book for postage (maximum postage required is £3).

NAME (Block letters) _____

ADDRESS _____

_____